The Architecture of John Nash

Wm BEHNES S^c 1831

JOHN NASH
1752 – 1835

ARCHITECT

TERENCE DAVIS

THE ARCHITECTURE OF
John Nash

INTRODUCED WITH A CRITICAL ESSAY BY SIR JOHN SUMMERSON

STUDIO : LONDON

First published in 1960 by Studio Books (Longacre Press Ltd), 161 Fleet Street, London EC4, and printed by Balding & Mansell Ltd, Wisbech. The text is set in Caslon type and the blocks were supplied by Gee & Watson.

Printed and made in England

Contents

PREFACE   *Page* 7

INTRODUCTION BY SIR JOHN SUMMERSON   9

COUNTRY HOUSES AND CASTLES   21

SMALL HOUSES, COTTAGES AND FOLLIES   69

PUBLIC BUILDINGS   89

PALACES, TOWN HOUSES AND METROPOLITAN DEVELOPMENTS   99

INDEX OF BUILDINGS ILLUSTRATED   137

PLANS   138

FRONTISPIECE: John Nash, 1831. A bust by William Behnes, enlarged by Cecil Thomas and set under the portico of All Souls', Langham Place, London in 1956. Photographed by Hans Wild.

TO MY MOTHER

Evelyn Grace Davis

Preface

THIS BOOK is an attempt to provide a true visual record of John Nash's works in a form that clearly shows his great creative powers and range of talents. I have purposely included nearly all his known works — good and bad — and the result is therefore not a personal selection but a full and, I hope, faithful picture of his achievements. I have balanced this with a text in which I have tried to weigh up the merits and defects of each building.

The fact that Nash built in more styles and moods than any other architect before or since his time has made it difficult for me not to use almost every adjective — both complimentary and derogatory — to describe his works. So varied and of such diverse qualities are his buildings that at one time it almost seemed plausible to divide the book into such sections as 'Bizarre', 'Scholarly', 'Gloomy' and 'Inventive'. In 1808, for instance, he designed a ponderous Gothic castle in Co. Durham, a radiant Italianate villa in Surrey, and added a fantastic, pinnacled wing to an ancient house in Staffordshire. All three buildings are entirely different in style and mood and yet clearly by the same hand, heart and mind.

During the past hundred years or so Nash's world has fast been disappearing and strangely enough this has little to do with the architect's ever-censured methods of building. Although time has certainly indicated that most of the surviving London terraces require constant repair (and in some cases complete renovation), it is also the tough, stone-built castles that have come to grief. Many of these great Gothic mansions lie neglected and abandoned, open to the skies of England and Ireland, whilst others have been demolished. Vanished too, in the name of development, are the little villas, once charming landmarks on coast-line and river bank.

When I first started to prepare the material for this book I intended to use every existing photograph, drawing and engraving, but as my researches grew it become clear that the material available on Regent Street alone would fill a volume of this size. Some of the photographs were repetitive, some unsuitable for reproduction and others lacking in special interest. I have collated, however, much new and hitherto unknown material although faded photographs must in some cases serve as historical records of demolished buildings. I have included plans of buildings where the exteriors, as often happens, tempt us to see inside. The dates, unless otherwise stated, refer to the commencement of building. Works illustrated are described in numerical order in the text preceding each section of plates, with the exception of [1, 2 and 183] which are mentioned in the introduction. *All numerals in square brackets refer to illustrations.*

My main source of reference and inspiration has been Sir John Summerson's biography *John Nash: Architect to George IV.** On reading this absorbing adventure-story I became so

---

*Allen and Unwin, London, 1935. Second edition 1949.

(7)

tantalised by descriptions of works that were not illustrated that I set out to build my own collection of pictures and they now form the nucleus of this book.

I would like to record my special thanks to Sir John for allowing me to borrow his rightful subject, for his valuable advice and for the pleasure I have had in discussing the whole project with him.

I am also grateful to the many owners of houses whose kindness and hospitality have made my researches possible. In this respect I would like to thank The Viscount Gort for his particular help and generosity.

My work has been greatly assisted by the Crown Commissioners, the Commissioners of Public Works in Ireland, The National Trust; the Trustees of: The British Museum, The London Museum, Sir John Soane's Museum; the Librarians of: The Royal Institute of British Architects, The National Library of Wales, The National Library of Ireland, The William Salt Library, The Gloucester City Library, The Worcester Public Library, The Brighton Corporation. Miss Ann Cox-Johnson, Librarian in charge of The St Marylebone Local History Collection, has also given most rewarding advice and I am particularly indebted for much help from Mr Cecil Farthing, Deputy Director of The National Buildings Record.

When in Ireland I could not have covered so much ground but for the enthusiasm of Mr Barry Mason who took several photographs [81, 82, 83, 84, 98, 100, 101, 102] and motored me many hundreds of miles to examine remote buildings. I would also like to thank Mr Herbert Felton whose advice proved invaluable on visits to several houses and whose work is shown in [31, 33, 34, 35, 36, 75, 77, 78, 79, 80]. The following photographers have also made valuable contributions: Mr A. F. Kersting [155, 159, 165], Mr Bernard Mason [15, 86, 87, 88, 89], who drew my attention to the drawing reproduced in [85], Mr Edwin Smith [16], Mr Start Walter [3, 4, 5, 6, 93, 96], Mr Gordon McLeish [90, 149, 152]; [44] is reproduced by permission of *The Belfast News-letter*. [60, 61, 62, 192, 193] are reproduced by permission of *Country Life*. The *Radio Times* Hulton Picture Library provided several pictures. Mr Donald Insall, ARIBA, supplied [69, 70].

The photographs on the cover and [161, 163] are by Major E. L. Paske whose work I was fortunate enough to discover in the archives of the St Marylebone Local History Collection and by whose kind permission they are reproduced. Mr Rex Smith patiently waited for traffic to abate in order to photograph the important buildings shown in [182] and [183] and speedily copied material in the possession of several of the museums acknowledged above.

Among the many industrious correspondents who have supplied information and other material I must especially thank the following: Mr F. S. Green, Librarian of the County Seely Library, Isle of Wight; Mr F. H. Booth, ARIBA, County Architect, Isle of Wight; Mr Patrick Gwynne, ARIBA; Miss M. Wight. Mr I. Wyn Jones has allowed me to make use of material from his excellent thesis on Nash's work in Wales and Mr E. M. Jope of Queen's University, Belfast, has supplied me with information on houses in Northern Ireland.

To Mrs Jacqueline Kennish I owe my warm thanks for her efficient and faithful assistance in collecting material from many obscure sources, and finally to Mr Richard Slawson, ARIBA, for drawing the plans.

TERENCE DAVIS
27 Park Crescent, London.
Spring 1960

Introduction

BY SIR JOHN SUMMERSON

MR NASH is a very clever, odd, amusing man', wrote Mrs Arbuthnot after a visit to East Cowes Castle in 1824, 'with a face like a monkey's but civil and good humoured to the greatest degree.'[1] Bits and pieces from other sources accord with this. Lawrence, in the portrait at Jesus College, Oxford, irradiates the monkey-face with wisdom and charm; but Nash's own description of his 'thick, squat, dwarf figure, with round head, snub nose, and little eyes'[2] is at once more truthful and more expressive of his own idea of himself as a tough old customer taking the world as he finds it, delighted with its rewards, uncomplaining of its kicks. He was amusing, as Mrs Arbuthnot says: his personal letters are spontaneous and racy. He was most phenomenally clever; and 'odd' perhaps in the sense that, living in a world where many of the more showy attributes of success were within his reach he retained a single-minded passion for one thing above all others — architecture. Architecture as his own original creation; architecture as an artistic gamble; and, best of all, architecture achieved in highly speculative projects, with big money and sharp wit.

He had the defects of his merits. As a man of business, though he was no rogue, he moved sometimes a little too fast to be wholly respectable. As a designer he certainly moved much too fast to be respectable at all by the standards of the scholars and critics of his own or any other time. His detailing was terrible. And, what is worse, he knew that it was terrible and did not care. 'Never mind', he would say of some egregious misfit arising from one of his sketches, 'it won't be observed in the execution.'[3] Of course it was and will continue to be observed. It cannot be helped; and any critic who attempts to reconstruct a Nash façade on orthodox lines will find to his dismay that the correction of minor faults merely leads to the exposure of major ambiguities and thus to the devaluation of the whole. Nash's broad scenic genius is a thing in itself.

Much of Nash's work, including every single house in his famous street, has been destroyed. But, ironically, the very first buildings he ever built in London — buildings which represent an early and disastrous failure — have survived. At the corner of Bloomsbury Square and Great Russell Street is a big house ([183] formerly two houses), now the premises of the Pharmaceutical Society.[4] This, with the row of smaller houses adjoining, was built or remodelled by Nash as a speculation in 1777-78 when he was twenty-five. He failed to sell the houses and in 1783 was declared bankrupt. He disappeared to Wales and only emerged to begin a new career after ten years of provincial oblivion, by which time the Bloomsbury episode had, for all practical purposes, been forgotten.

This early group of town houses, isolated in time from all Nash's other work, is most instructive. Without the assurance of documentary evidence one might date them a generation ahead of their time; yet in fact they belong virtually to the era of Portland Place and

Bedford Square, when all London building was following in the wake of Robert Adam. Clearly, in these all-stucco houses whose Bloomsbury Square façade was a reversion to Inigo Jones's posthumous gallery at Somerset House and whose Roman ornaments contained not one single element from the Adam repertory, Nash already envisaged the London style he was later so magisterially to impose. Indeed, the next time he drew upon Jones's classic theme was at a strategic point in Regent Street itself.

The young man who so rashly tried to seize architectural leadership as well as financial profit in one speculative gamble had, in 1777, very little behind him either in cash or influence. Born in 1752, the son of a Lambeth mill-wright who died when he was nine, he had worked his way through the office of that able and affluent Palladian, Sir Robert Taylor. He had a well-to-do calico-printing uncle and may possibly have been connected with the more elevated Nashes of Worcestershire; but his London environment was certainly rather dim at the time of the bankruptcy.

We follow him to Wales. Nash's Welsh period belongs roughly to the years 1783-95: inside dates are mostly wanting. He settled in Carmarthen, where his mother seems to have had connections; he operated as an architect and builder, he acquired some land, and mixed and play-acted with the small gentry of the county. Houses traditionally associated with him in Carmarthen are not altogether acceptable as Nash designs and are no doubt mere property developments. Only in 1789 does he emerge as a real architect with the building of Carmarthen gaol. This had a stone façade which anybody might have designed who knew how Sir Robert Taylor designed stables; it was followed by a smaller gaol at Cardigan and a larger at Hereford [137], all now demolished. The country houses of the period begin, equally, with derivatives from Taylor. Foley House, Haverfordwest, is a rather impoverished imitation of Taylor's Coptfold Hall, Essex. Ffynone [49] is similar but with a square plan and the pedimented elevation repeated four times. Llysnewydd [66] breaks away from this model and seems to owe something to the architectural country box with which John Soane, Nash's future rival, was experimenting and specimens of which he had published in 1788.[5] Nash's more exciting and more personal houses were still to come.

The great thing about the Welsh period is not so much the gaols or the country houses as Nash's initiation into 'the Picturesque'. Exactly how this came about may some day emerge, but we have enough evidence now to know that round about 1794 he was in close touch with a group of west-country personalities who, at that moment, were revolutionising the English attitude to landscape as well as considerably modifying the English idea of the country house. Perhaps the first contact was with Colonel Thomas Johnes, the translator of Froissart and creator of the romantic domain of Hafod. Nash worked for Johnes's father at Cardigan and for the son he built an octagonal library at Hafod in 1793. Now Johnes's wife was a relative of Richard Payne Knight of Downton; and Richard Payne Knight's wife was Ursula Nash, with whom it is not at all inconceivable that John Nash claimed some remote relationship. Another friend of Johnes's was Uvedale Price, Payne Knight's neighbour at Foxley in Herefordshire and the man with whom he was sharing his new ideas on aesthetics. Price employed Nash to build him the Gothic and triangular Castle House at Aberystwyth some time in the early 1790's.[6] So it is beyond dispute that Nash was in the midst of this circle of romantic, scholarly, innovating land-owners. It is equally beyond dispute that he adopted their views; the whole of his later career proves it.

The Picturesque, as a theory, really belongs to Uvedale Price who postulated it as a category outside of and complementary to Burke's celebrated categories, the Sublime and the Beautiful.[7] It involved an attitude to nature and thus to landscape-gardening and, in turn, to architecture within landscape. Payne Knight, who accepted Price's theory in a general way, held very distinct views on this latter aspect and had, in fact, put them into practice at Downton where, still in his twenties, he built himself a house in 1774-78.[8] Downton is of the utmost importance in the story of John Nash for one can see at a glance that it is a close relation of his long series of castle houses; its early date shows it to be their prototype.

Downton is a long, irregular building with octangular and square embattled towers, obviously intended to give something of the impression of an Edward I castle. This exterior, however, is deceptive for inside we find a series of rooms on a single axis all designed in a most finished Classical style and including (in the square tower) a magnificent miniature Pantheon. This duality was adopted by Knight to make his house conform externally with the wild and rugged landscape of Downton Vale and internally with the civilised requirements of an eighteenth-century gentleman. Nash was to do the same in many of his houses. His own house at East Cowes [41], for instance, borrows Downton's octangular and square towers — and its interior was originally entirely Classical.

But it was not only from Downton that Nash learnt the precepts on which his success was to be based. Both Payne Knight and Uvedale Price believed that landscape should be studied through the eyes of the great landscape painters, notably of Claude. It followed that the architect should observe the kinds of buildings depicted in these landscapes and strive to combine their irregular silhouettes with the requirements of modern domesticity. Nash accepted this challenge and there is a series of country houses by him, including Cronkhill and Sandridge [15 and 76], where the Italian effect is manifest — and manifest through Claude.

If Payne Knight and Uvedale Price inspired and directed Nash's first experiments in the Picturesque, there was a third party to whom he was from a practical point of view even more indebted. This was Humphry Repton, the landscape-gardener. Repton was exactly Nash's age — which is to say that in 1794 they were both forty-two. Like Nash, he had a rather patchy career behind him but had quite suddenly turned the corner into success by assuming the mantle of 'Capability' Brown, who had died in 1783, and figuring as the great landscapist of the age. Repton's views were not at all those of his great precursor; they were, on the other hand, very close to those of Knight and Price. Wild nature was to be respected, not groomed Brown-wise into a pre-figured harmony. The 'true character' of a scene was to be evaluated and enhanced and, in the process, architecture was to play its part. The rebuilding or alteration of the house was nearly always essential to a Repton improvement. Hence Repton required constant architectural aid and meeting John Nash in the circle of Knight and Price, a perfect initiate of the Picturesque, it was natural that a partnership should suggest itself. From about 1795, Repton was regularly introducing Nash to his clients, receiving in return a percentage on the architect's fees. Repton's eldest son joined Nash's office in 1796, a younger son following him a few years later.

While it lasted, the partnership was an enormous success, and it lasted for some seven years. Then in 1802 there was a quarrel, arising it seems from Nash's failure to recognise the artistic contributions made by Repton's eldest son, John Adey Repton. Thereafter, the landscape-gardener and John Adey worked together. Nash worked alone, though with the younger Repton, George, continuing in his office as a draughtsman. It was no hardship to

Nash who by 1802 could very well dispense with Repton. The association had brought him full into the world of wealth and elegance, and had even brought him to court, for in 1798 he had been able to exhibit at the Royal Academy 'A Conservatory for H.R.H. the Prince of Wales'. Whether it was built we cannot be sure, but it was the first service rendered to the Prince by the man who was to build him two palaces and, under his aegis, to transform his capital.

Nash's country house career extends altogether from about 1792 till 1812 when it was cut short by the descent of his prodigious London responsibilities. During those twenty years he rebuilt or remodelled something like forty houses in England, Wales and Ireland, as well as designing innumerable lodges, cottages, dairies, farms and stables. They are the output of what should have been his best and most creative years. What are we to make of them?

Nash houses are the product of a quick wit and an uncommon but not infallible flair for putting the right thing in the right place. Some are strikingly original; others flatly repetitive. A Nash house never merits prolonged study: it is seen at once to be a success or a flop. If it is a success the success will be in great part due to good siting and a witty choice of style. Choice of style was a great factor and by style the houses are most easily divided.

The few Classical houses demand more serious consideration than the others since, being bred in Classical ways, Nash had some of the proper technical equipment. The earliest Classical houses derive, as we have seen, from Taylor. Southgate Grove [29], however, is something rather new. Planned round a grand double staircase, it has a garden front strongly recalling the house Robert Adam built for Dr Turton at Brasted, Kent — a house Nash will certainly have known. The Adam trimmings are, however, classicised away and the result is one of striking novelty, accented by French pots, sphinxes and oval windows. Even more original was the Casina at Dulwich [57] where Nash contrived a high circular domed pavilion between two low wings — an unheard-of composition for an English country house and with something in it, perhaps, of the Comte d'Artois' 'Bagatelle' in the Bois de Boulogne.[9] He developed the same idea at Rockingham in Ireland [47] but as neither has survived one cannot now judge of his success.

The castles are another thing altogether. The castellar elements from Downton are disposed this way and that, built usually in rough stone of the locality with very few and very crude medievalist frills. Their plans tend to include a long range of reception rooms, linked somehow to a portentously long gallery. A conspicuous external success is Caerhayes in Cornwall [63] where the site lends itself generously to an operatic performance of this kind. The vanished Ravensworth [12], a castle of enormous size where the landscape did not much help, one remembers only with boredom. Siting is all-important for the castles. Where it does not positively assist, the Nash castle tends to slump into a rather forbidding jumble of none-too-evocative elements. The whole idea of the sham castle is wrapped up with the idea of romantic landscape, as Repton — and, indeed, Nash — well knew. On the flat, a castle needs to exert itself as an architectural composition with more force than Nash had the inclination to supply.

There are other sorts of houses. One, of very special importance, is the kind which may be Gothic as at Luscombe [59], castellar as at Killy Moon [25], or peasant (Claudian) Italian as at Cronkhill [15], but whose plan is fairly constant — an irregular disposition of rooms round a staircase, sometimes allowing for a built-in cloister or loggia. This small, compact, irregular type of plan, successor to the rambling Gothic plans of James Wyatt, constitutes in fact the first stage in a kind of English villa planning which continued far into the nineteenth century.

There are stylistic oddities — Jacobean as at the demolished Hale and Tudor as at Longner [85]. And finally there are the cottages — the peasant architecture of England pressed into the vocabulary of the landscape artist. In this sphere Nash did extremely well, mastering the intricacies of gables, hips and thatched bonnets in a way which Norman Shaw and Nesfield might have envied. The still existing group at Blaise [116, 117] summarises the whole affair and is one of the most interesting products of the architecture of the Picturesque.[10]

At sixty, Nash was still a country-house architect, liberally patronised by rich vulgarians, and himself something of a vulgarian and passably rich. He was married to a brassy beauty with no brains, twenty-one years his junior. He had a smart house in Dover Street [180] and an estate in the Isle of Wight, with a castle at East Cowes of his own improvisation. In certain circles which revolved round Carlton House he was a great success; he thought of going into Parliament. At this stage his career might well have dissipated itself into a retirement full of dinner-parties, political fencing and the scandals of two courts. But it did nothing of the kind. At sixty, Nash entered upon the main architectural commitments of his life.

The story of Regent's Park and Regent Street as official building projects of the Crown goes back to 1793. In that year an award of £1,000 was authorised for a suitable plan for laying out the Park. This money was eventually collected by Nash but exactly what went on between 1793 and 1806, when he was appointed architect to the Commissioners of Woods and Forests, nobody knows. Even after that appointment, four years elapsed before he was officially instructed to make a plan at all, though it is evident that the Regent's Park idea had been growing in his mind for some time. This is proved by the existence of two long panoramic sketches for buildings in and around the Park, buildings which do not connect with any known plan and which must be earlier than 1810.[11] A curious thing about these panoramas is that they were drawn by a Frenchman, who not only left a few words in French on one of them but gave some of the buildings a more French look than Nash's own buildings ever have. The likely answer is that the Frenchman concerned was Charles Augustus Pugin, a refugee from the Terror who had been in Nash's service since the Welsh days, and who very likely abetted his francophile leanings.

Now the French elements not only in these sketches but in the whole conception of Regent's Park are important, but they are closely interlocked with traditional English elements and it is convenient to consider these first. At the outbreak of war in 1793, London town-planning stood in a very promising way. The owners of large estates on the outskirts were considering how to break away from the monotonous criss-cross of the built-up areas and attract people outwards by open suburban developments conceived in the style of Bath. Almost the only surviving example of this tendency is the much-admired Paragon at Blackheath, a crescent in which the houses are built in pairs, linked by colonnades; but the same kind of development was seriously considered in 1794 for St John's Wood and about the same time for Camden Town.[12] Proposals for these areas included circuses, crescents and squares but allowed at the same time for the building of detached villas and rows of semi-detached houses with any amount of open space. Unfortunately these schemes were scotched by the adverse economic conditions of the early war years and when the revival came after 1815 were found altogether too generous in their plot ratios. Nash, nevertheless, kept the Bath tradition well to the fore in approaching the Park problem. The double circus he planned for the high ground in the centre is an obvious theft from the St John's Wood scheme of 1794; there is Park Crescent [143]; and the terraces with their highly architectural symmetry derive ultimately from John Wood's north side of Queen Square, Bath.

The Regent's Park conception was, however, far more than a continuation of this excellent native tradition. It possessed the character of an independent urban unit — almost (in its early form — Plan 1) of an ideal city. There was to be provision for all classes of the community, with a palace for the King, barracks for the armed forces, a great church, villas for the nobility, terrace-houses for the middle classes, and a working-class marketing area to which supplies were to come by canal. All these features except the palace were in fact executed, though the self-contained and 'ideal' character of the Park was gradually dissipated as it was overtaken by the natural outward growth of London. Nevertheless, Regent's Park cannot be explained without some inquiry into the lofty and dramatic comprehensiveness which characterised its beginnings. England of Nash's time had no tradition of new towns, still less of ideal cities. Whence, then, came the inspiration?

The answer may well be Ledoux. In 1804 there appeared in Paris the spectacular folio entitled *L'Architecture Considérée sous le Rapport de l'Art, des Moeurs et de la Législation*. Claude-Nicolas Ledoux had been a successful architect before the revolution. Then after twelve years of unemployment he found himself commissioned by the French government to lay out the salt-manufacturing town of Chaux, near Besançon. To this project, which was partly executed, he attached a programme for a *ville sociale*, a programme combining the utmost Utopian liberalism with architectural visions of corresponding extravagance. This is the main subject of his book. The whole production has a wild, irresistible beauty and modern critics have not been slow to compare it with Le Corbusier's Utopian projects of the 1920's. If we may take it that Ledoux's book came into Nash's hands in or soon after 1804 it is not improbably the source of that feeling for the play of social factors as determinants of design which informs the original Regent's Park project and makes it something wholly new in the history of English town-planning.

Naturally, there were no politically liberal fantasies in the Regent's Park plan. There were some oddities, however. It was odd to call the Regent's proposed palace a *guinguette*—a French expression of doubtful origin and slightly dubious meaning. It was even odder to propose to erect, in the middle of the double circus, a *valhalla* — something on the lines of the Pantheon. This proposal first appears in the 1809 Report of the Surveyor General of Land Revenues and did not necessarily originate with Nash. But as the first *valhalla* so called was the one begun by Ludwig of Bavaria near Regensburg in 1830 its appearance in a British state paper of 1809 is very curious indeed.

Neither the *guinguette* nor the *valhalla* was, of course, ever built; but their original inclusion illustrates the romantically adventurous way in which the Park was imagined. It was to bring the Picturesque to town and match it against the Heroic. The villas (some fifty of them) were to stand half-hidden in groves and Repton's doctrine of 'apparent extent' was to be cultivated by liberal planting at strategic points in the enclosure. Repton, of course, was absent from Nash's counsels at this period but the Park would have owed much, and still owes a little, to his influence.

Regent's Park today [Plan 2] is a very fragmentary and dissolute reflection of the brave image of 1812. In the absence of the villas (only eight were built, and only one, the Holme, survives in anything like its original form) the terraces have it too much their own way. But some of their façades, so atrociously detailed and poorly built, are among the most entertaining improvisations of their time. Take Cumberland Terrace [141], designed with special pomp to face the Regent's *guinguette*. Nash's thought here probably started from the correct and sensitive but curiously timid river front of Somerset House by Chambers. The Four Courts at Dublin and Newgate Prison also leave their mark, but the Terrace transcends them all in sheer architectural excitement. It was a brilliant thought to reduce Chambers's Palladian bridges to triumphal arches (compare the Four Courts), linking the main blocks, and leading to little courtyards beyond. Chester Terrace [164] is as original but more serene. In its three porticos we catch a fleeting recollection of Versailles; in its triumphal arches we see perhaps a highly apposite conversion of those in Palladio's Villa Pisano. But Nash's sources are often disputable. How are we to account for Cambridge Terrace, a façade broken by a recessed centre, with ornaments in the Soane style above and, below, Vignolesque cinctured columns formed into three porticos to bring the duality to heel? And what of Sussex Place [150]? This very odd creation can be connected with a rejected Nash design for a royal palace but it has been much simplified. The ten 'towers' are really nothing but bay windows of a kind which Nash learnt to do in Taylor's office, continued upwards to pointed octagonal domes whose rear portions are self-supporting. From other designs by Nash we can interpret them as an attempt to create a classical equivalent for Elizabethan corner towers such as may be seen at Burghley or Hatfield.[13] This issue, however, is very successfully obscured by the interminable 'Louvre' colonnade threading through the whole composition.

Other terraces are less recondite. York Gate [158], which frames St Marylebone Church, is a *vis-à-vis* rearrangement of Gabriel's two blocks in the Place de la Concorde, reduced to a tiny scale. While Park Crescent is a simple English crescent, rendered exceedingly striking by the neat expedient of linking all the porches into one unbroken Ionic colonnade.

Park Crescent leads us out of the Park and towards its companion masterpiece, the Street. A new north–south artery had always been considered an essential corollary of the Crown's development of Marylebone Park and at least two schemes had been suggested before Nash, in 1813, submitted three new proposals and estimates, one of which was accepted by the Treasury. The selected plan was something very like the street as finally executed, at least so far as the line of street was concerned. The architectural conception must have changed considerably as the hard economic facts of site-disposal made themselves felt.

Old Regent Street can now only be studied in prints and photographs [169-79]. But the line of the street is there, and in that still living artery of London Nash's authority and ingenuity are felt every day. Any Londoner knows that Regent Street is not effectively crossed at any point between Oxford Circus and Piccadilly; he knows that to turn eastwards out of Regent Street is to enter the shabby half-light of Soho while to turn west is to be at once in 'the west end'. This is because Nash chose to cut his street exactly where the Soho network met the more spacious criss-cross of the west-end estates. He was thus able quite literally to buy his property in Soho and sell it in the west end; while another calculated result was to keep disreputable Soho firmly in its place.

This choice of line may be thought to have been a matter of economic expediency rather than of aesthetics and so, no doubt, it was. But architectural repercussions were immediate and challenging. At the north end, Nash had elected to start his street with the existing Portland Place. The Portland Place line had to meet the main Regent Street line at

(15)

Oxford Street and it did so at an angle. Four main streets meeting at odd angles demand some contrivance to separate the entries: hence Oxford Circus.[14] At the south end there was a more considerable difficulty. The street was to terminate with a formal avenue and *place* on the axis of Carlton House. This axis, produced northwards to Piccadilly, missed by a long way the main Regent Street line. Nash, therefore, swept this line round eastwards in a quarter of a circle, cutting the Carlton House axis just north of the crossing of Piccadilly: hence the Quadrant [178] and hence also the remarkable composition formed by Piccadilly Circus [179] with the County Fire Office [176] to the north terminating the vista from Carlton House.

During the progress of the Street two further factors served to modify its shape still more. A hitch occurred (the details are too complicated to give here) in the acquisition of land in line with Portland Place. The Street had to have a kink. There was no possible alternative and Nash made a virtue of it. He persuaded the Church Commissioners to take some of the adjoining ground and there built them a church with a circular vestibule and steeple exactly in the kink, the church itself running dutifully to the east, unseen, the vestibule forming a terminal feature: hence All Souls', Langham Place [128]. Finally, when George IV had determined to build Buckingham Palace, Carlton House, which had been the *terminus ad quem* of the original project, was declared redundant. It was torn down and Nash planned the Duke of York's Steps, the two Carlton House Terraces [187] and Carlton Gardens on the site of the old palace and its grounds.

This brings us to the actual architecture of the old street taken as a whole. It is as well to remember that, as originally designed, it terminated at the south in front of a palace. Waterloo Place [176] was conceived as approximating to a *cour d'honneur* for Carlton House; indeed, the buildings overlooking it on the north had inverse affinities with the Ailes Gabriel at Versailles. The strict formality here was answered by the formality with which the County Fire Office, crowned by a figure of Britannia, saluted Carlton House from the high ground beyond Piccadilly Circus. The whole of this southern part of the street was of imperial address. And when Carlton House came down, Nash still maintained the regal theme in the Duke of York's Steps and the two tremendous terraces which turn their colonnades towards the Park and flank the processional way to the Palace.[15]

Then the Quadrant. The Quadrant could only have occurred to an Englishman, steeped in the circus and crescent tradition of Bath. The words 'circus' and 'crescent', in their urbanistic application, are English inventions: so is the analogous 'quadrant'. The Quadrant was simply a quarter of a double circus; the monumental Doric colonnades which, till 1848, projected over its pavements, were nothing more than an aggrandisement of the simple idea contained in the linked porches of Park Crescent. Waterloo Place, Lower Regent Street, Piccadilly Circus and the Quadrant, then, further north, Oxford Circus and the terminal All Souls' — these were the formal elements of old Regent Street. For the rest, there is one word which explains, and forgives, a great deal — improvisation.

The improvisatory character of much of Regent Street was a direct outcome of the economic difficulties which the project encountered in its most critical years. The Street, it must be remembered, was not built by the government with government funds. It was built by a Commission under Act of Parliament with borrowed money. It was a commercial undertaking. Certain symmetries were imposed but not always could blocks of sites be disposed of exactly to conform with the blocks of architecture which the architect deemed most appropriate to the grand perspective. Thus, in the main stretch of the street, between the Quadrant and All Souls', façade succeeded façade with curious inconsequence. There would be a long grand front and then a few narrow nondescripts, then a long façade again, then perhaps a church, and so on. Picturesque is, of course, the word; and in this context a significant one. The grand façades were mostly designed by Nash himself but it would be a mistake to claim too much for them as architecture. He did not take the shop-front problem seriously into account; it was perhaps too novel for him to envisage as a problem at all. And he designed the blocks very much as if they were sides of squares — symmetrical rows of houses, with decorated centres and ends. Only a few of them had the sense of adventure we find in the Park. Nevertheless, as a whole the Street fell into a series of far from disagreeable perspectives, the casual and accidental always controlled by the ballast of the larger and more architectural blocks. In his report Nash had mentioned the High Street at Oxford (an 'accidental' collocation of colleges, houses and churches) as an admired prototype and we can see very well what, as an inspired student of the Picturesque, he learnt from it. The notion of the Picturesque, indeed, provided the only possible solution for a street built piece-meal and continually bedevilled by the exigencies of the estate market.

In Nash's London work as a whole there were, it will be seen, three main sources of inspiration. First, the English town-planning tradition as exemplified in Bath and its derivatives. Second, the public works of Paris and Versailles, from Louis XIV to Napoleon. Third, the theory and practice of the Picturesque. But Nash's sources never quite explain him. He is always reaching for something entirely original, something which will shock by its novelty if not by its complete artistic success. His invention was sometimes naïve, as when he erected for the Peace celebrations of 1814 a bridge across the St. James's Park canal with a pagoda on top of it [140]. But when, in the following year, he started adding to the Pavilion at Brighton [1], he produced a building with some real strokes of architecture. The onion domes and the minarets are, to be sure, mere oriental souvenirs; but the Banqueting Room [2] and the Music Room are apartments of an original kind, successfully worked out, and more beholden to Classical tradition than to anything out of India or China.

The London works end with two extraordinarily different enterprises. One was the layout and design of the Park Villages, a model suburb planned with serpentine roads on either bank of the canal at the north-east corner of the Park.[16] This was a deliberate return to the idea embodied in Blaise Hamlet, the idea of cottages designed singly and in pairs to produce a varied and effective architectural picture. In the Park Villages, the cottages have become middle-class houses — Italian, Gothic, Tudor and Swiss. They are the prototype of all Picturesque suburbia [90, 93-97].

The other undertaking — ill-omened and ultimately disastrous — was Buckingham Palace [189].[17] The instructions to convert and enlarge Buckingham House were given in 1825 and Nash produced a design as sensational as anything he had done. Underlying it one can discern the influence of Sir John Soane's Royal Palace project, shown in the Academy of 1821. Nash followed Soane in articulating every part of his composition and attempting thereby to give it movement and a provocative silhouette. A dome, pavilions rising into attics, turrets, and detached fore-buildings to terminate the wings: such-like elements were designed to catch and delight the eye, as indeed they do in the solitary engraving we have of the original design. If the façade of Cumberland Terrace (designed about this time) merely adumbrates a vast palace, here was a palace proper in three dimensions conceived with the same rash invention. Alas! in execution it was a total failure. The improvisatory genius of

Regent's Park and Regent Street could not, at seventy-three, settle into the course of serene concentration necessary for the achievement of a monumental successor to Hampton Court and Greenwich. At the Parliamentary Inquiry of 1828, even Nash admitted that he had blundered.

It was the end of his career. In 1829, a Select Committee sat to consider his conduct; in 1830 he was dismissed and, George IV being dead, the Palace works were stopped, to be continued, with radical revisions, by Edward Blore. Although every charge of dishonesty or mechanical incompetence fell to the ground, there was no question that Nash was in disgrace. He had taken as sudden a fall as he had when his Bloomsbury adventure failed, half a century before — and from a much greater height.

But the old man was not unduly perturbed. He retired to East Cowes and lived, for another five years, a well-ordered, extremely comfortable and amusing life. By and large he had done exceedingly well and as the loyal servant and friend of George IV he passed into the shadows in very remarkable company. On 13 May 1835 he died in his castle and was buried in the graveyard of the little church across the park.

1. *The Journal of Mrs Arbuthnot* 1820–32 (ed. F. Bamford and the Duke of Wellington, 1950), entry for 29 August 1824.

2. Nash to Soane, 18 September 1822. A. T. Bolton, *The Portrait of Sir John Soane* (1927), p. 353.

3. C. J. Mathews, *Life of C.J.M.* (1879), vol. i, p. 252.

4. The building was somewhat altered for the Society in 1860 when the window pediments and attic storey were added. The dentil cornice was hacked off the smaller houses in Great Russell Street in 1951.

5. J. Soane, *Plans, Elevations and Sections of buildings . . . in various counties* (1788). Soane's influence on Nash, throughout the latter's career, was important though rarely obvious.

6. E. I. Jones, 'An Eccentric's Castle House', *Country Life*, 4 July 1952, p. 33. T. J. L. Prichard, *The New Aberystwyth Guide* (1824), p. 11. W. Bingley, *Excursions in North Wales* (1839), p. 179. In English eighteenth-century architecture triangular plans with corner towers go back to W. Halfpenny, *A Complete System, etc.* (1749), pl .44. The triangular Longford Castle (sixteenth century) is engraved in *Vit. Brit.*, v (1771), pls. 94–98.

7. The best account of the movement is C. Hussey, *The Picturesque* (1924).

8. N. Pevsner, 'Richard Payne Knight', *The Art Bulletin*, xxxi, 4 December 1949.

9. Equally, Nash may have been prompted here as so often, to go one better than Soane. The villa with a domed centre bay had been common in England since Wyatt's Heaton Hall (1772). Soane, in his design for Burn Hall (*Plans, etc.*, pls. 34 and 35) and elsewhere added an attic storey to the bay. The Ionic wings may well derive from another Soane design (*Plans, etc.*, pl. 40). However, 'Bagatelle' is still a likely source for Nash when designing a 'Casina'.

10. Blaise Hamlet, as the group is called, is now the property of The National Trust. J. Summerson, 'Blaise Hamlet', *Country Life*, 14 October 1939.

11. Recently transferred to the Public Record Office. L.R.R.O. 1/1051 a and b.

12. J. Summerson, *Georgian London* (1945), p. 158; *Heavenly Mansions* (1949), p. 105.

13. See the two designs for remodelling Carlton House, reproduced in H. Clifford Smith, *Buckingham Palace* (1931), pls. 24 and 25.

14. Nash's own rationalisation of this use of the Circus (which derives from French park planning) was that it diminished the impression of Oxford Street forming a boundary between two districts of different social character.

15. The Carlton House Terraces, built in 1827, are of course the most obvious of Nash's debts to Paris, recalling as they do Gabriel's palaces in the Place de la Concorde.

16. Park Village East, the more extensive of the two, was more than half destroyed by a late Victorian enlargement of the railway cutting. 'Gothic Cottages' and 'Ionic Cottages' among other groups were swept away and no records of them appear to exist. However, the surviving houses at the north end are certainly the earliest and the most likely to be associated personally with Nash. The canal was filled in about 1945.

17. For the building history of Buckingham Palace see the section by Christopher Hussey in H. Clifford Smith, op. cit.

The above introduction is largely based on the author's *John Nash: Architect to George IV* (1935; 2nd. ed. 1949) to which the reader is referred for general reference. The notes given here mainly refer to sources not used in that work.

2   THE BANQUETING ROOM, ROYAL PAVILION, BRIGHTON

Country Houses and Castles

NASH'S HOUSES AND CASTLES are his most important contribution to British architecture and are apt to be forgotten under the overwhelming impact of the more familiar London terraces and street architecture.

It is in these houses that we see the man as a creative architect, unharassed by the political maze surrounding the grandiose schemes of the Prince Regent. Here is no speculative builder, no town-planner but a successful architect whose talents led him into the good graces of illustrious landowners at the end of the eighteenth and beginning of the nineteenth centuries. Before he plunged irrevocably into the London scene he left behind him a score of mansions in various styles many of which had great merit and all of which are worth recording if we are to get a true picture of his career.

Although Nash professed to dislike working in the Gothic style he built no fewer than twelve large Gothic mansions. Romantic Gothic was the order of the day and Nash obeyed it. When he deserted country house building he never again used Gothic detail in any important scheme. The Regent's Park terraces and Regent Street bear witness to this even though Gothic terraces were springing up in Cheltenham, Birmingham and elsewhere. The reason probably lies in the fact that, in his own words, 'One window takes more trouble in designing than two houses ought to do.' The plans for London did not allow for such time-consuming attention to detail.

The castles are not castles in the real sense. They are stone-built castellated mansions with Gothic detail but often with Classical interiors. Some are heroic and beautifully sited, others dull and brooding but all combine to make an impressive picture of Nash's struggle to produce the Picturesque Ideal on a grand scale. His use of pretentious castellated turrets and towers to give an illusion of grandeur was exactly the reverse of the procedure adopted for his design of the *cottages ornées*, an expression invented *c.*1795 by John Plaw. Moderate mansions were made to resemble vast castles and small country houses were dressed like tiny cottages.

The large stuccoed Classical houses are a different story and the best of them place Nash high on the list of distinguished architects. The worst have no greater faults than those of the light-hearted use of architectural elements and careless (but sometimes endearing) application of Classical detail, hitherto employed with awed scholarship. But the villa-style houses are in their way wholly successful and their elegant stuccoed façades and graceful interiors cannot fail to please even the most academic of critics.

Of the eight large houses Nash built in Ireland not one remains inhabited and most are total ruins. The Welsh houses are smaller and several are in good repair. In England three castellated mansions have been demolished, one has been destroyed by fire and two are semi-derelict. Because of their moderate size, three villa-type houses are well cared for and in the hands of people who have happily carried out only the most sympathetic alterations.

SOUTHBOROUGH PLACE, Surrey. 1808.

[3–7 and Plan 3]. *An L-shaped stuccoed villa built for Thomas Langley in the old parish of Ditton.*

This most charming villa comes as a surprise to those who see it for the first time, surrounded as it is today by modern houses and situated in a suburban road. The property originally included considerable park-land, stablings and other out-buildings. These still exist but are used as separate units [5 and 6]. The angle of the L contains an octagonal porch with copper dome. The south elevation is wholly satisfying and the balustraded bay window is a feature which Nash learned to use when working with his old master Sir Robert Taylor. All the first-floor windows are round-headed and the decorative supports to the broad eaves can be compared with those used on several other houses, such as Cronkhill and Sandridge [15 and 76].

The interior features are Classical and include an oval stone cantilever staircase with S-balusters, fine marble fireplaces ([7] shows an original drawing from George Repton's notebook), attractive feather and acanthus cornices, and fluted architraves. The drawing-room and dining-room are intercommunicating and have large double doors.

The villa, now called Southborough House, is well cared for by its present owner, Dr N. A. Power.

WEST GRINSTEAD PARK, Sussex. *c.*1806.

[8–10]. *A large castellated house built for Walter Burrell, a younger son of the Sussex historian.*

The site, un-Sussex-like in its flatness, has a wild romantic air with turf and bracken growing close up to the house. It was built of limestone cut to the size of bricks and, in its original form [9], it must have been very picturesque. Ill-conceived additions of the 1860's shown in [8] robbed the house of its plain, grim outline.

The double-return Gothic staircase [10] was the most arresting feature of an interior that contained a circular dining-room and other rooms having Gothic details of a graceful, naïve kind. Two of the main bedrooms contained good chimney-pieces — one of white and lavender-coloured marble and another in richly carved white marble.

The house which now belongs to Lord Glendyne is unoccupied and semi-derelict.

RAVENSWORTH CASTLE, Co. Durham. 1808.

[11–14]. *An ambitious Gothic house, designed for Sir Thomas Liddell, a member of a successful industrialist family.*

The house was built on the site of an earlier Georgian house in which were incorporated two thirteenth-century towers. The exterior (north front [12] and west front [11]) must have always presented rather forbidding elevations, but the interior was interestingly planned and contained a monumental Great Hall or gallery in the romantic medieval style with a grand staircase, timber roof and nine tall, transomed windows [13]. There was also a Gothic library with pinnacled bookcases and vaulted ceiling supported on corbels [14]. With Nash's apparent lack of interest in Gothic detail, it is possible that Augustus Pugin, his assistant, supplied some of the drawings for Ravensworth.

The castle, once used as a school, was enlarged and altered in the 1840's, fell into decay and was demolished in 1953.

CRONKHILL, Shropshire. c. 1802.

[15–17 and Plan 4). *Most Italianate of all the houses, built for the agent to Lord Berwick of nearby Attingham.*

Beautifully sited on a gentle slope looking towards the Wrekin, the house is romantic and informal. It relies for its effect on the massive round tower linked to a lower square tower by a slender-columned colonnade. The chimney-stack piercing the roof of the round tower would be amusing in a smaller house or cottage, but here spoils the satisfying composition of curve against horizontal line. Chimney-stacks were carefully omitted from the original drawing (in Sir John Soane's Museum) submitted to the client [17]. The round tower is merely a dramatic architectural trick and does not contain, as one might hope, a spectacular circular staircase nor even one circular room.

The house, owned by Colonel E. N. Thursby, has recently been repaired and re-painted.

SHANBALLY CASTLE, Co. Tipperary. c. 1812.

[18-24]. *A great Gothic composition, built for the Earl of Lismore, the work carried out by A. Hargreaves*

The exact date of this design is not known. The original drawings at the Royal Institute of British Architects ([20] shows south front) are undated, but it has much detail in common with Lough Cutra and was probably designed at a time when Nash was too busy with his schemes for London to visit Ireland and supervise the building. The entrance front [19] was not especially interesting but more impressive than Lough Cutra. The south front however was most spectacular, the round and hexagonal towers at each end forming sturdy 'stops' to the great run of Gothic windows and tracery of the conservatory.

The interior was Gothic and most of the details were well considered. There were important marble chimney-pieces in the Gothic taste [23 and 24]. The entrance hall (known as the gallery), was vaulted and lit by a series of rose-shaped lights. A great archway led to one of Nash's most splendid double-return staircases with a vaulted Gothic ceiling of much refinement [21 and 22]. The dining-room was

hexagonal and connected to an oval drawing-room by a square ante-room. From the drawing-room a series of rooms, including the library and conservatory, stretched along the south side, ending in two smaller hexagonal rooms. There were other rooms on the ground floor of considerable size.

The house has been unoccupied for a considerable time, the fittings have been removed and complete demolition work is in progress.

KILLY MOON CASTLE, Co. Tyrone. 1803.

[25, 26 and Plan 5]. *A small castle built for Colonel William Stewart whose family had held the property since the seventeenth century.*

This is a smaller and more pleasing version of Kilwaughter Castle and its plan, containing rooms of elliptical, octagonal and square shapes, was to be used by Nash in various forms in many of his larger country houses. A drawing in George Repton's notebook [25] shows a romantic, moon-lit composition with every window arched, and every tower and wall castellated. The realisation of this dream [26] was not quite so endearing and the castle must have looked somewhat stark and gloomy. The interior contained details in polished oak which were in naïve but inventive Gothic taste.

The house cost £80,000 to build and was sold a few years ago — as a total ruin — for £100.

GARNSTONE, Herefordshire. c. 1806.

[27, 28]. *A large Gothic house in green sandstone built for Samuel Peploe.*

This ponderous pile was one of Nash's least successful attempts to create a picturesque Gothic mansion. The whole composition was clumsy and ill-conceived, although the contemporary engraving shows it to have been well sited in pleasant surroundings. The interior contained a spacious staircase hall lit by a large lantern with traceried windows of a pedestrian design.

The house was demolished in 1959.

SOUTHGATE GROVE, Middlesex. 1797.

[29–36]. *An early stucco-rendered Classical villa with stone Ionic columns, built for Walker Gray.*

This pretentious but beautiful house seems at first sight to be large but is, in fact, a skilful essay in creating an illusion of grandeur on quite a small scale. Never again was Nash to take so much care over the correct use of the orders and this house might well be described as his most scholarly tribute to neo-Classicism. The house contains an important double-return staircase and the drawing-room, library and crescent-shaped conservatory were *en suite* so that all three rooms could be thrown into one. The conservatory has been demolished.

The entrance vestibule [34] contains unusual painted panels depicting classical figures [36] and an attractive radial-fluted and vaulted ceiling supported on decorative corbels. To the left is a very pretty octagonal room known as the Bird Cage Room containing exceptional panoramic landscape wall paintings. The staircase hall [35] rises the whole height of the house and has a great rectangular lantern, the shape of which has been altered. An acanthus leaf cornice [33] runs round the hall under a coved ceiling. The house, although built in the grand manner, contains not one single important chimney-piece, all of them being of a very perfunctory design.

Before Southgate became an overblown suburb of London, the house was surrounded by exquisite park-land, landscaped by Repton. The remnants of the grounds now form a public park and the house is at present used as a convalescent home known as *Grovelands*.

ATTINGHAM, Shropshire. 1810.

[37, 38]. *A picture gallery for Lord Berwick.*

The gallery was designed to accommodate the works of art that the second Lord Berwick had collected in Italy. 'Porphyry' scagliola Corinthian columns and pilasters frame alcoves at each end and the apartment is top-lit by a deep, glazed cove above the cornice. An original drawing [38] shows the cove to be filled with oval lights but this was not carried out. Nash also designed a circular staircase with fluted walls at this time.

The house is now owned by The National Trust.

EAST COWES CASTLE, Isle of Wight. c. 1798.

[39–42 and Plan 6]. *Nash's own Gothic mansion.*

This house, situated on the brow of a hill overlooking sloping park-land to the sea, was Nash's favourite hobby and country retreat for over thirty-five years. He built several other houses and public buildings on the Isle of Wight including the Guildhall, Newport, the Isle of Wight Institution and the Marine Villa.

The walls inside the staircase tower were fluted and the staircase itself typical of one of Nash's circular cantilever designs. The dining-room had rich details, the cornice being fluted and enriched with a motif of tassels and curtains painted red and gold. The fireplace was of black marble with brass mounts. The drawing-room was decorated in Paris Directoire style, had a cavetto cornice with gilt anthemion and a white marble fireplace with Egyptian figures. The library was a mixture of Gothic and acanthus details, painted in red, blue, green and gold. The octagon room had a radial-fluted circular ceiling which still exists. It was in these splendid surroundings that Nash entertained the

Prince Regent in 1817. Many alterations were made over a period of years, including the addition of the long conservatory, the massive octagonal tower on the north-east and another storey over the drawing room. The ashlar masonry was well-executed and clearly Nash could continue adding and subtracting to his heart's content. The total effect of the composition was one of irregular, rugged grandeur and an extra tower or turret only enhanced its picturesque shape. The long gallery ([39] shows an early photograph) was removed wholesale from Nash's house at 14 Regent Street [40 and Plan 15] — a double mansion so designed that Nash's living accommodation was planned on the first floor and virtually formed a flat.

The castle later passed into the hands of the Vereker family who commissioned Nash to build Lough Cutra on somewhat similar lines in Co. Galway. It has now fallen into almost complete decay, stripped of its fittings and was recently robbed of the woodwork and masonry of the long conservatory. The property now belongs to Mr Arthur Guy.

AQUALATE HALL, Staffordshire. 1808.

[43]. *The only example of a large stuccoed country mansion in Gothic style, forming an elaborate addition to an existing house belonging to Sir John Fenton Boughey Fletcher.*

Aqualate's picturesque name comes from the nearby Mere, the largest natural sheet of water in the county. The pinnacled buttresses and castellated parapets achieved a rich and fantastic effect, prophetic of the bays and domes of Sussex Place.

All Nash's work was destroyed by fire in 1910.

KILWAUGHTER CASTLE, Co. Antrim. 1806.

[44 and Plan 7]. *A Gothic mansion built for Edward Jones Agnew incorporating a seventeenth-century castle.*

This composition is in the West Grinstead-Knepp tradition [9 and 72] and gains its effect from the massive round tower and the grouping of smaller towers and turrets. The Gothic window-tracery was built up as wooden frets inserted into the window embrasures outside the window-frames themselves. The frets were feeble in construction and must have always required constant repair. The most curious exterior details were window-sill carvings in sandstone, carried out by a local craftsman of some skill and originality. The entrance porch, unhappily crouching to the west side of the round tower, leads to an inner vestibule and thence to a half-octagonal staircase hall. The hall contained semicircular alcoves, one of which gave access to a circular drawing-room. The interior details were mostly shoddy — the staircase hall was panelled with openwork Gothic tracery of thin wood. The dining-room contained vaulted plaster spandrels with restrained fluting.

The house was occupied by the Agnew family until the outbreak of the Second World War, was stripped of its fittings in 1951 and now lies a disintegrating shell.

KENTCHURCH COURT, Herefordshire. c. 1795.

[45]. *An older house remodelled for John Scudamore.*

Nash, when he was becoming known in the West and the Midlands, gladly accepted remodelling commissions from the established gentry and his work at Kentchurch can be compared with additions and alterations made at Ingestre, Corsham, Bulstrode and elsewhere. He was responsible for the fine drawing-room in the new wing and generally reshaping a rambling series of buildings of various dates.

The house, recently seriously damaged by flood, is still privately owned by the Lucas-Scudamore family.

ROCKINGHAM, Co. Roscommon. 1810.

[46, 47]. *A Classical house built of limestone for Robert Edward King, First Viscount Lorton of Boyle.*

Rockingham was one of Nash's finest Classical houses and the only one in this style built by him in Ireland. (Casina at Dulwich [57] built thirteen years earlier somewhat resembles it and is a humbler version.) It stood in a commanding position overlooking a lake and magnificent countryside.

Three domed bays lit the interior of the house and the plan was formed round these features. There was a circular library with a parlour and drawing-room on either side and a bedroom suite was also situated on the ground floor with principal bedrooms on the first floor. A fire severely damaged the house in 1860 but in 1822 the whole composition had been ruined by the addition of two extra storeys and the removal of the dome [46]. The house was restored to its 1860 look and some of Nash's plans were used for reinstating the interior but the entire building was finally burnt down in 1957.

The drawing [47], probably by George Repton, shows the original composition and is in the possession of Sir John Summerson.

WHITSON COURT, Monmouthshire. c. 1795.

[48 and Plan 8]. *An early Palladian house of brick with stone dressings.*

Whitson is one of the very few Classical houses not faced with stucco. Plain and quite handsome in appearance, the exterior house shows none of Nash's later inventiveness. The

staircase, however, is unusual and rises to the first floor only, and is lit by a dome in the roof through a circular opening of equal diameter in the second floor. Some indiscriminate alterations to the fenestration of the east front have robbed the house of its scholarly composition.

The house, having been a convent during the early part of this century, is now once more in private hands.

FFYNONE, Pembrokeshire. 1793.

[49–54 and Plan 9]. *A Classical house built for Captain Colby.*

Ffynone was perhaps the most successful of Nash's early houses — quite plain, well-mannered and with a great sense of style. The plan is simple but the interior contains much interesting detail, most of it surviving a later grandiose remodelling of the house. The vestibule has an attractive vaulted ceiling [52] and an archway in the inner hall [53] has a circular fanlight repeating that of the main front door [51, 54]. The semi-circular staircase has refined S-balusters. One of the three identical elevations ([50] shows one) was upset in the 1820's by the addition of a Greek Doric forebuilding [49], and the whole exterior was given an expensive 'face-lift' by Inigo Thomas in 1904, who added keystones to every window and over-loaded the walls with heavily rusticated quoins.

The house is still a private residence.

THE KING'S COTTAGE, Windsor. 1814.

[55]. *An elaborate* cottage ornée *designed as a country retreat for the Prince Regent.*

Royal Lodge, or The King's Cottage as it was first named, was no more a cottage than the Royal Pavilion at Brighton was a bathing hut. It was estimated that the retreat cost £200,000 to build, furnish and equip, and although this estimate may be exaggerated, it emerged more of a palace than a cottage. Nash designed it in picturesque style with thatched roof, a thatched verandah, cast iron conservatory and many other rustic details. The interior contained marble chimney-pieces and Princess Lieven, who stayed there, found 'in everything a habit of unspoiled magnificence, which left behind the sentiment of *une charmante béatitude*'. It was, in fact, a small palace that happened to be thatched.

Little of Nash's work remains today in the building now known as Royal Lodge.

WITLEY COURT, Worcestershire. c. 1805.

[56]. *Alterations for Lord Foley.*

Nash's impressive Ionic portico has survived a fire that gutted this great country house in 1937.

CASINA, Dulwich. 1797.

[57]. *A Classical villa for Richard Shawe, solicitor to Warren Hastings.*

Shaw paid for his villa out of the proceeds of the Warren Hastings trial and like Southgate Grove, this was one of Nash's early, more successful exercises in Classical design. With its round pavilion and Ionic flanking wings, the composition was effective and was complemented by Repton's landscaping.

The house stood in an elevated position overlooking the rural village of Dulwich and commanded extensive countryside views. At the time the house was described as 'a convenient and elegant structure — light, airy and superb'. An ornamental canal, part of which still remains, was planned to flow through neighbouring estates to provide a picturesque feature in the surrounding land, but this was never executed.

The house was demolished in 1906 and [57] from J. Hassell's *Views of Noblemen and Gentlemen's Seats in the Counties adjoining London* (1804), is a rare pictorial reference.

CHILDWALL HALL, Lancashire. 1806.

[58]. *A castellated house built for Bamber Gascoyne, Member of Parliament for Liverpool.*

One of the least interesting of the large houses, Childwall none the less had some inventive features. It was built of red sandstone and had a striking overall silhouette, somewhat similar to Knepp [72]. The interior had Gothic details and the library contained ingenious shutters which disappeared into the walls.

The house eventually passed to the Marquis of Salisbury, was more recently a golf club and has now been demolished.

LUSCOMBE CASTLE, Devonshire. c. 1800.

[59–62]. *A castellated house designed for Charles Hoare, the banker.*

Repton was first on the scene here and introduced Nash to design a house 'blending a chaste correctness of proportion with a bold irregularity of outline' to complement his own commission to landscape the grounds. The result was picturesque and pleasant but the original plan did not allow for the ponderous bay window [59] which was added by Nash to the garden front shortly after completion of the house and appears as a clumsy afterthought. Most of the interior details are Classical and the fine staircase, lit by a large Gothic window, has Nash's favourite S-balusters [62].

The house is owned by Sir Peter Hoare, Bart.

CAERHAYES CASTLE, Cornwall. 1808.

[63–65]. *A Gothic house built for John Bettesworth.*

Caerhayes is probably the most successful of the romantic castles built in the Gothic taste and commands magnificent views of park-land and Cornish seascape. The building is tough and rugged in appearance, and it is interesting to remember that Nash designed Southborough [4], entirely different in character, in the same year. The massive round towers are most effective and the whole composition sits well against its background of fine woodlands. The stable courtyard, a later addition, is designed to conform to the character of the main house and is approached by a broad stone arch [65]. An unflattering contemporary engraving [63] shows the castle as a dark, brooding composition. Although Gothic externally, the interior details are a mixture of Gothic and Classical. On the ground floor a long vaulted hall, top-lit by a galleried opening, leads to an impressive double-return staircase behind a broad arch supported on Classical corbels. This combination of detailing is quite acceptable and gives a less sullen effect than the similar Gothic galleries of Lough Cutra and Shanbally. The remainder of the interior contains Classical mouldings of a modest nature.

The house is owned by Mrs M. Williams.

LLYSNEWYDD, Cardiganshire. c. 1795.

[66–68 and Plan 10]. *A stuccoed Palladian house built for Colonel Lewes.*

This pleasing house was square in plan and without visible out-buildings. The oval windows with delicate web glazing were to be used later in grander schemes such as Southgate [29] and Dover Street [180]. In Victorian times the house suffered a fate even worse than demolition at the hand of an 'improver'. Gone are all the simple Classical features and today the house is completely unrecognisable [68]. The interior, too, has been similarly mutilated, the fine semi-circular staircase replaced by a monstrous Victorian construction of wood and most of the original details removed.

DOLAUCOTHI, Carmarthenshire. 1792–95.

[69, 70]. *A remodelling of an old house for John Johnes.*

The owner was not a rich man and asked Nash how he could restore and improve his house without completely rebuilding it. For £436 Nash provided a new façade facing the park-land transforming a typical farmhouse building into a stylish mansion. The new front was merely a theatrical screen [69] but today the disguise seems good value for the money. The bay windows are a later addition.

The house is now derelict but the property belongs to The National Trust and the park-land is maintained.

SION HOUSE, Tenby, Pembrokeshire. c. 1790.

[71]. *A three-storied house built for William Routh, a printer of Bristol.*

The exact date of this curious house is not known, but in

style it appears to be earlier than Nash's other square-planned houses and possesses a distinctly metropolitan air. It was built on a prominence and could be approached from both sides by an imposing carriage drive. A great bay window rose the whole height of the house on both main sides and these were treated as curved walls within.

The building was elaborated in the Italian style in the late nineteenth century and destroyed by fire in 1936.

KNEPP CASTLE, Sussex. 1809.

[72–74 and Plan 11]. *A Gothic mansion built for Sir Charles Burrell, Father of the House of Commons.*

Sir Charles Burrell was apparently so pleased with Nash's work for his brother at West Grinstead [9] that he commissioned him to design Knepp. The two houses have something in common although Knepp is more grandiose and less compact. The entrance front [72], is impressive with its four identical towers. The whole composition is cement-rendered and sited in picturesque park-land containing a lake. The out-buildings are formed round a courtyard to the north-west and the large round tower contains a circular staircase with Gothic window [73].

In 1904 a severe fire destroyed much of the interior, since restored and somewhat altered. The house is owned by Sir Walter Burrell, Bart.

SANDRIDGE PARK, Devonshire. 1805.

[75–80 and Plan 12]. *A stuccoed Italianate villa built for the widow of the first Lord Ashburton.*

Few houses are situated more splendidly than Sandridge, placed high on the bank of the river Dart with lawns sweeping away to the south and west. Until recently the house was protected on three sides by thick woodland, but this was almost entirely destroyed a few years ago by a timber merchant who owned the property for a short period. The prospects from the house however are unimpaired and of great beauty.

The villa much resembles Cronkhill [15] but is somewhat more spread out, although still quite compact. The exterior relied for much of its charm on the pretty trellis details of the conservatory and bow window [76] but whereas Cronkhill still possesses the solid, time-resisting feature of its stone colonnade, Sandridge's Egyptian-style trellis columns of wood have all vanished save one on the bow window. The conservatory has been demolished and the archway seen in [77], forming a new entrance to the house, replaces it.

But even with these important details missing the round and square tower elements make up a dramatic composition. The plan was curious. The original front door (now removed) led into an attractive octagonal arched vestibule [80]

with double doors leading directly into the drawing-room. The staircase is found in the corridor at the north-west end of the drawing-room, access to the corridor from the front of the house being only through a narrow door concealed in one of the vestibule arches. The corridor is vaulted as is the bedroom corridor above [78] and the staircase has an unusually wide round-arched window [79]. The dining-room which is contained in the round tower has a dark grey marble chimney-piece of the same design as one at Southborough [7] and the cornice — acanthus leaves wrapped on to a plain round moulding — in this room and in the drawing-room is also identical with that at Southborough. There is a charming round room at the top of the tower with oval windows. All the interior details are pleasing and much use has been made of splayed windows soffits, chamfered angles to walls and corbelled vaulting. The house is undergoing restoration and sympathetic alteration and The Earl Cathcart, the present owner, preserving all surviving original features.

LOUGH CUTRA CASTLE, Co. Galway. Before 1817.

[81–84]. *A Gothic limestone house built above the shores of Lough Cutra for the Right Hon. Charles Vereker, Member of Parliament for Limerick.*

Apparently Vereker, who became Lord Gort in 1817, so much admired Nash's own house, East Cowes Castle [41] that he commissioned him to provide a similar one in this remote and beautiful part of western Ireland. The castle has magnificent views across the Lough to unspoiled and richly wooded country and its tough construction proves that not all Nash's houses were flimsy.

The offices and gardens were created on areas blasted out of solid rock and the green sward from the house to the lake was artificially constructed. The grim but noble exterior is somewhat similar to East Cowes but its compact plan was spoiled in 1856 when the house was greatly enlarged by the addition of a new wing to the east ending in a clock tower seen in [84]. At this time the castle was owned by Lord Gough of Goojerat fame who plastered the walls of the main rooms with wallpaper bearing the initial letter 'G' and added military trophies such as the grouped cannon balls on one of the lodges and in the stable courtyard [82]. Both Dog Lodge and Limerick Lodge [125] were almost certainly designed by Nash and have none of the clumsiness of the later additions to the house.

Unlike East Cowes, the interior is entirely Gothic and has much in common with Shanbally. The rectangular entrance hall is vaulted and at one end a broad arch leads to the staircase well in the round tower seen in [84]. The staircase [83] is Gothic and of oak, and although pleasing, considerably less spectacular than most of Nash's castle staircases. It leads to the bedroom landing which is lit by three circular domes.

The drawing-room and dining-room are *en suite*, linked by a vaulted ante-room originally containing great double doors.

The drawing-room has a rich Gothic cornice, but the original marble chimney-piece has been replaced by a crude arrangement in stone. Two alcoves at the north end of the dining-room once contained decorative wood and plaster-work, but this now has been removed. Not one original chimney-piece remains in the main rooms and several of the smaller marble chimney-pieces from the bedrooms have been removed to the stables, now used as a separate residence.

The castle is semi-derelict and has not been lived in since 1922, but happily it is once more in the hands of the Gort family. It is the intention of the present Lord Gort, who has already removed some later additions, to restore Lough Cutra to its unique place in domestic architecture.

LONGNER HALL, Shropshire. 1806.

[85–89]. *A house in elaborate Tudor taste built for Robert Burton, one of Repton's clients.*

The old house was pulled down in 1803 and Repton considered Nash's proposals to rebuild to be in the wrong style of architecture and also badly sited. However, the house was built as planned and it is the only surviving example of Nash's flamboyant essays in a Tudor style. The house contains a fine staircase hall, the stairs starting in one flight and returning in two. There are exaggerated fan-vaulted ceilings in the hall [89] and corridor. The library [87] also has a vaulted ceiling and the dining-room [88] a Gothic cornice. [85] shows the loggia on the south front to have been open with a conservatory as a separate unit to the east.

The house is owned by Mr Richard Burton.

3 SOUTHBOROUGH PLACE, SURREY

4

5

SOUTHBOROUGH PLACE, SURREY

6

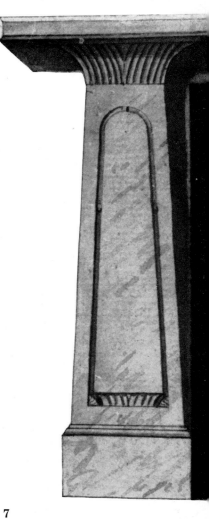

7

8

WEST GRINSTEAD PARK, SUSSEX

9

10 ▶

11

RAVENSWORTH CASTLE, CO. DURHAM

12

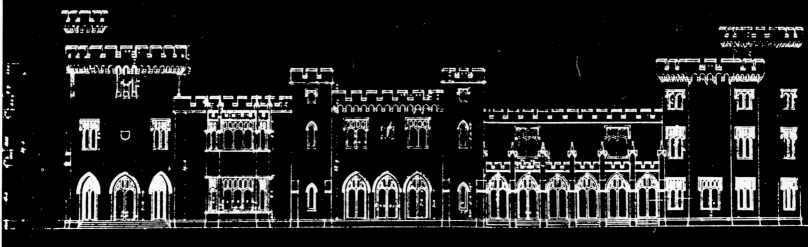

20

21   22

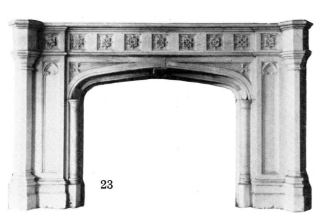

23   24

KILLYMOON CASTLE, CO. TYRONE

27

28

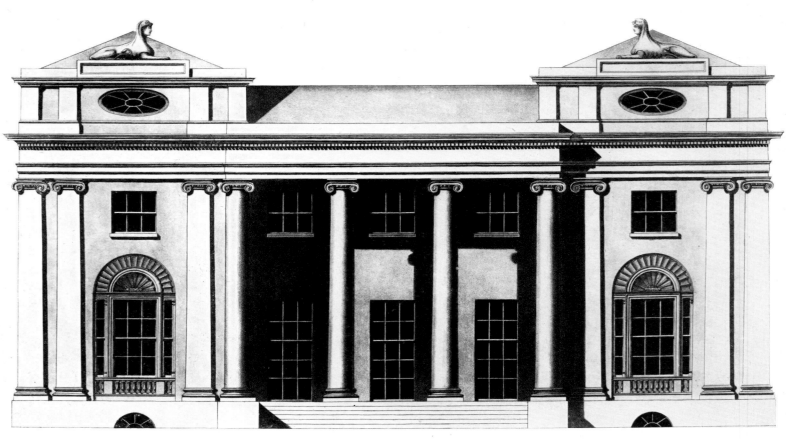

29

SOUTHGATE GROVE, MIDDLESEX

30

31

32

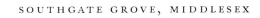

33

34 35

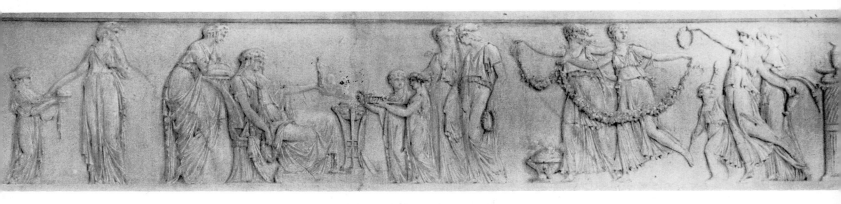

36

37

ATTINGHAM, SHROPSHIRE

38

39

EAST COWES CASTLE, ISLE OF WIGHT

40

41

42

43   AQUALATE HALL, STAFFORDSHIRE

44   KILWAUGHTER CASTLE, CO. ANTRIM

KENTCHURCH COURT
HEREFORDSHIRE

45

46   47

ROCKINGHAM, CO. ROSCOMMON

48

WHITSON COURT,
MONMOUTHSHIRE

49

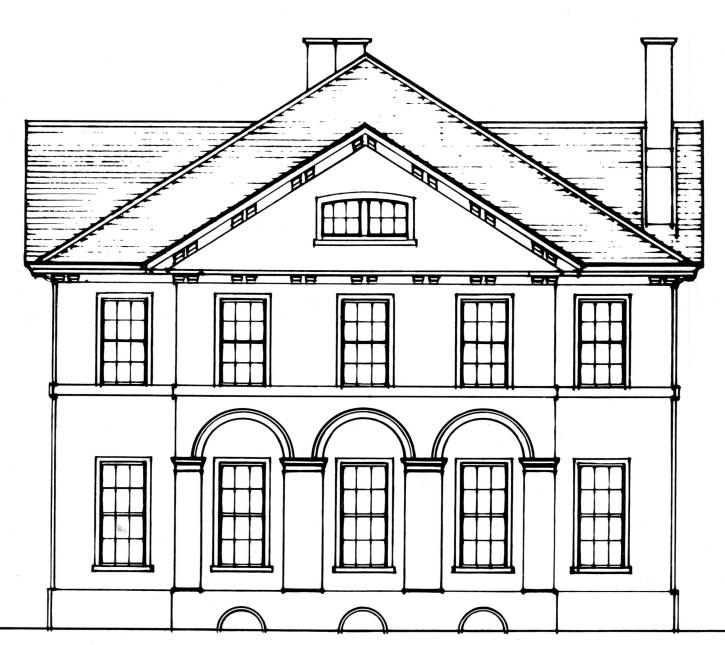

50

51

52

53

54

55   THE KING'S COTTAGE, WINDSOR

56   WITLEY COURT, WORCESTERSHIRE

57   CASINA, DULWICH

58   CHILDWALL HALL, LANCASHIRE

59

60

61

62 ▶

63

CAERHAYES CASTLE, CORNWALL   65▶

64

66

67

68

LLYSNEWYDD,
CARDIGANSHIRE

70

DOLAUCOTHI,
CARMARTHENSHIRE

69

71
SION
HOUSE,
TENBY

72

KNEPP CASTLE, SUSSEX

74

73

75   SANDRIDGE PARK, DEVONSHIRE

76

77

SANDRIDGE PARK, DEVONSHIRE

78   79

80

83

84

85

86

LONGNER HALL,
SHROPSHIRE

87

88

Small Houses, Cottages and Follies

DURING the early part of the nineteenth century a series of most engaging books were produced expounding the delights of picturesque cottage architecture. For instance, in 1805 Robert Lugar published a volume of coloured engravings and called it, somewhat cumbersomely, *Architectural Sketches for Cottages, Rural Dwellings and Villas in the Grecian, Gothic and Fancy Styles Suitable to Persons of Genteel Life and Moderate Fortune.* The text sets out all the snobbish ingredients of a 'genteel life' and the references to class barriers, elegance and taste would today put even the most patronising estate agent to shame. J. B. Papworth, who designed much of Cheltenham, offered a book of equal interest and charm — *Rural Residences* (1818). Again similar phrases are used and the words 'elegant refinement' and 'picturesque effects' help to show that the vogue for the little houses illustrated was more than a matter of architecture; it was a state of mind coddled by social changes. 'Domestic Economy' is even mentioned, but the economy often began and ended with a rustic porch sheltering the door to a lavish interior.

Surprisingly (and disappointingly) Nash did not produce his own book of small house and cottage designs although he was one of the main contributors to this particular art of picturesque deception. He was, for example, commissioned by his cousin to enlarge Rheola, a very small house near Neath, on the strict understanding that it should remain a small house in appearance. But this example of inverted snobbery was only stucco-deep as the new library alone was able to accommodate two hundred people for dancing. Nash's most notable exercise of this type was the King's Cottage at Windsor. Here all the rustic *cottage ornée* decorations were used — thatch, trellis, and dormer window — but the illusion was completely destroyed by great clusters of carved brick chimneys, obviously part of a large mansion.

Nash built a number of small houses, some in cottage style and others with Gothic and Classical detail, but unfortunately only those in the Park Villages in London have survived. The others, unprotected by the Crown as are the Park Villages, have been demolished or altered beyond recognition by subsequent owners. (The villa shown in [91, 92] is an example.)

He also designed several follies and ornamental buildings for the estates of country gentlemen who were thereby able to enjoy the fashionable pastime of showing their friends a new dairy disguised as a rustic cottage, a cow-house masquerading as a Doric temple or simply a Druidical 'ruin' set in dramatic surroundings. Often these attractive little buildings formed part of Repton's plans for landscaping the grounds and Nash invented them with ease and obvious delight. Most of the cottages he scattered over the West Midland estates and elsewhere are now as forgotten and neglected as his great country houses.

The Blaise Hamlet cottages fall mid-way between the deceptive *cottages ornées* and the follies. They were not, of course, intended for the 'genteel life' yet they were more than follies, being practical housing for tenantry. But they were designed in a style exactly in tune with the same romantic ideal — to translate the picturesque manner of the past into acceptable forms for the present.

12 PARK VILLAGE WEST, London. *c.*1830.

[90]. *A small Classical villa with octagonal tower. The first tenant was Dr James Johnson, physician to the Duke of Clarence. He also attended Nash.*

This little villa has many remarkable features and is the most entertaining in the Village. The east elevation contains a great bow rising the whole height of the house and is in complete contrast to the angular front elevation with its tower and heavily pedimented porch. The broad eaves, evocative of Southborough [3], are carried the whole way round the house at various levels. The bas-relief panel over the pediment is a later addition. The house contains a charming octagonal entrance-hall and graceful staircase with Gothic window.

The fabric has recently been completely restored and further accommodation has been added to the north by its present owner, Mr Woodrow Wyatt, MP.

VILLA AT LIPHOOK, Hampshire. *c.* 1800.

[91, 92]. *A whimsical villa built for Charles Taylor.*

Only drawings, from George Repton's notebook, can now give us a picture of this elaborate *cottage ornée*.

The capricious porch and mixture of pointed and round-headed windows, combined with delicate ironwork and thatched roof, made up the picturesque ideal demanded by a country gentleman of the time. The villa was completely remodelled at the end of the nineteenth century, although it retains three of the original main rooms. It is still a private house, now known as *Hollycombe*.

18 PARK VILLAGE WEST, London. *c.*1830.

[93]. *A small 'Tudor' house with bay windows and castellated porch.*

One of a group of houses in various styles with gardens forming an island site in the Village. This is one of the few surviving examples of a stuccoed house in Tudor style.

10 and 11 PARK VILLAGE EAST, London. *c.* 1824.

[94, 95, 97]. *A pair of semi-detached villas in plain Classical style.*

The pretty crenellated bargeboard saves this pair of houses from dullness. The houses back on to the old canal site and form part of the Park Village East group, now reft of more than half its houses by the railway cutting. These houses have been little altered over the years.

17 PARK VILLAGE WEST, London. *c.*1830.

[96]. *A small stucco Gothic villa.*

This house might be a miniature offspring of Aqualate Hall [43] and its pinnacles, pointed eaves and bay windows provide a lively contrast to the other plainer villas in the Village. Later additions to the porch have robbed the design of its crisp perpendicular effect and the ironwork retaining the garden has unfortunately been removed.

GRACEFIELD, Co. Leix. 1817.

[98–102]. *A small stuccoed villa with Gothic details situated in an elevated position in the former Queen's County.*

When Gracefield was built, Nash was busy with his great London developments and therefore sent the plans over to a Mrs Kavanagh for whom the house was executed by Robertson of Kilkenny. Neale gives us the following contemporary and thoroughly misleading description of the house: 'The original design of this picturesque and commodious residence was furnished by Mr Nash of London. . . With respect to the external architecture, the design has been much admired for that pleasing effect which a varied outline in buildings of this description seldom fails to create. The frequent breaks and strong projections in the walls, the cut-stone labels surmounting the windows and the general, though harmonious, irregularity of the whole produce an appearance strikingly animated and cheerful.' Cheerful the house may well have been, but commodious never. The other architectural features referred to exist but, in all, the house was never more than a charming little villa of no great distinction. Neale's engraving of the time [99] is as inaccurate as his description and shows the house with smaller central eaves and windows that never existed. We must assume that he made the drawing from Nash's original design which was modified later by Mrs Kavanagh. The entrance front still has its pretty cast-iron verandah to the left and right of a Gothic porch. 'Pebble-dash' now obscures the clean surfaces of the stuccoed walls, and the verandah and porch are entirely overgrown with creeper [98]. The garden front, also 'pebble-dashed', has a large bay window containing the dining-room and main bedroom. The verandah curves round to shelter the drawing-room window [100] and [102]. A Gothic conservatory leads from the dining-room [101]. A harsh terra-cotta balustrade now retains the terrace and gives the house an unsympathetic Edwardian flavour.

The plan is simple, the ground floor consisting of a square hall, staircase well, small rectangular drawing-room (about fourteen by ten feet), adjoining study and dining-room. The kitchens and other offices are found to the north of the staircase well. The interior details are unremarkable. None of the original chimney-pieces remains, several cornices have gone but the original fluted door frames still exist. The staircase sweeps in one curve to the bedroom corridor at the north end of which is an alcove containing two curved doors.

In spite of the fact that no major alterations have been made, the house is barely recognisable as the Regency villa it once was. Gracefield, now owned by Mr Robert Thompson, must rely for its charm on the beautiful gardens and countryside in which it is set.

POINT PLEASANT, Surrey. *c.* 1797.

[103]. *A small riverside villa at Kingston-on-Thames sometimes known as Bank Farm built for Major-General St. John.*

This exceedingly pretty Classical villa has long since vanished although the remnants of Repton's landscaping exists in the form of a few fine trees. It appears that the plan was square with bow windows facing the river, one of which was surmounted by a trellised verandah. Here Nash used semi-circular tympana over the windows, a device he was to include in many later buildings.

A MARINE VILLA, Cowes Parade, Isle of Wight. *c.* 1825.

[104]. *A Gothic sea-side villa built for Sir John Coxe Hippisley, Bart.*

The property consisted of a small stuccoed house with a separate ball-room or pavilion. When George IV stayed there it was described as 'an elegant Gothic residence'. The house passed into the hands of the Cust family where much entertaining was done in Edwardian times when Cowes society was at its height.

The Royal Corinthian Yacht Club now owns the house which is now completely buried in the depths of overbuilding of later years.

LISSAN RECTORY, Co. Londonderry. 1807.

[105 and Plan 13]. *A small Italianate villa built of rubble with pale buff sandstone dressings.*

This attractive villa is a less successful attempt to combine the round and square tower elements used at Sandridge and Cronkhill a few years earlier. The round tower, pleasing in itself, is set too far away from the main building to form a completely satisfactory composition but even so it has a picturesque rambling north elevation.

The drawing-room has three French windows with splayed soffits leading on to the loggia. The study is octagonal and the dining-room, the largest room in the house, rectangular. Some original fireplaces survive on the first floor and the house, still occupied privately, has been little altered inside.

The covered balcony over the loggia on the south front is a later addition and detracts from the effect of the stone arches below.

BLAISE HAMLET, Gloucestershire. 1803.

[106–117]. *A group of nine cottages in various styles.*

These romantic *cottages ornées*, built for J. S. Harford of Blaise Castle, form a *précis* of Nash's favourite diversion — cottage design — several of which he had already dotted over other country estates. The front doors of the cottages face away from each other 'to minimise local gossip' and the whole group sits primly round a village green. The designs are all different and each cottage was given a picturesque name: Vine [107], Oak [108], Sweet Briar [109], Dial [110], Circular [111], Jessamine [112], Rose [113], Double [114], and Diamond [115]. Dial Cottage has particularly attractive carved brick chimneys [106].

The Hamlet is now owned by The National Trust.

THE DAIRY, BLAISE CASTLE, Gloucestershire. c. 1803.

[118, 119]. *A picturesque building in cottage style.*

The original drawings from George Repton's notebook show the dairy as a crisp, neat little design set against a dramatic background of brooding trees. The finished result, however, was no more than a pretty 'Devonshire' cottage, sweeter but less substantial than the later cottages of Blaise.

The dairy still exists and is in good repair.

SKETCH FOR A NEO-TUDOR LODGE (undated).

[120]. *An original sketch by Nash in the possession of Sir John Summerson.*

This sketch may have been made in 1800 when Nash was producing ideas for the restoration of Helmingham Hall, Suffolk. At the bottom Nash has written 'George — make a fair drawing of this to 1/8 scale'. 'George' would be George Repton (see page 11).

LODGE, WHITSON COURT, Monmouthshire. c. 1795.

[121]. *A stuccoed cottage with open portico.*

This represents an early attempt to develop the picturesque cottage style and although there are few of the later Blaise Hamlet characteristics here, the open portico and heavy bargeboard are features that Nash was to use in various forms for many years.

DAW'S LODGE, MOCCAS, Herefordshire. c. 1805.

[122]. *A stone-built cottage with Gothic features.*

One of the several cottages or lodges designed for the Moccas estate.

BRIDGE LODGE, MOCCAS, Herefordshire. c. 1805.

[123]. *A red-brick lodge in rustic style.*

This is one of several cottages designed for the estate of Sir George Cornewall who had family connections with nearby Garnstone, also by Nash. This lodge is in the Blaise Hamlet tradition and resembles several cottages there.

ORNAMENTAL TOWER, CAERHAYES CASTLE, Cornwall. 1808.

[124]. *A terrace feature for John Bettesworth.*

This tower is a round version of the one Nash built for himself at East Cowes Castle and was designed to carry the eye from the main building to the landscape beyond.

LIMERICK LODGE, LOUGH CUTRA CASTLE, Co. Galway. c. 1815.

[125]. *A stone-built Gothic cottage on the Limerick Road border of the castle estate.*

It is almost certain that Nash designed the two main lodges at Lough Cutra and probably other cottages on the estate. The lodge is inhabited but the drive is no longer used.

A DRUIDICAL TEMPLE, BLAISE CASTLE, Gloucestershire. 1803.

[126]. *A proposed folly.*

This sinister temple, conceived by Nash and Repton, was never constructed but formed part of the proposed scheme for improvements to J. S. Harford's estate.

The drawing is enlarged from George Repton's notebook.

HOUSE

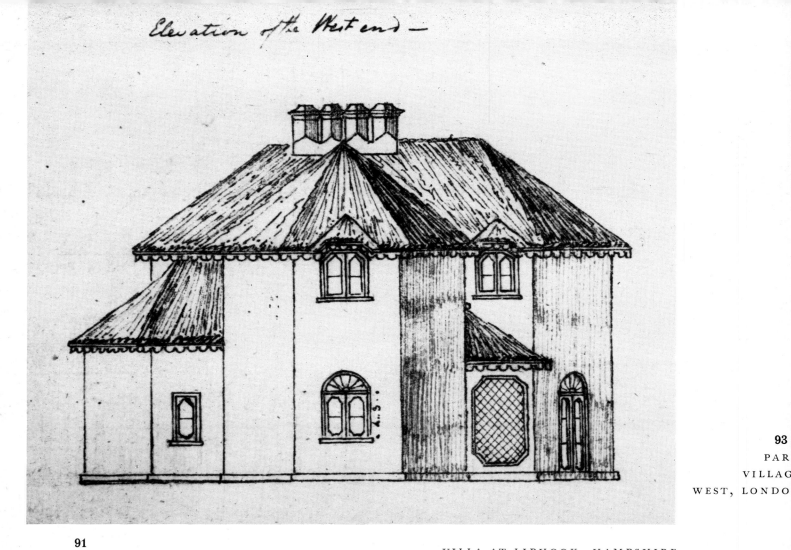

Elevation of the West end —

91

VILLA AT LIPHOOK, HAMPSHIRE

92

Ch. Taylor Esq.
Liphe

94

PARK VILLAGE EAST, LONDON

95

96

PARK VILLAGE WEST, LONDON

PARK VILLAGE EAST, LONDON

97

98

GRACEFIELD, CO. LEIX

99

103 POINT PLEASANT, SURREY

104 A MARINE VILLA, COWES, ISLE OF WIGHT

106 ▶

BLAISE, GLOUCESTERSHIRE

105

LISSAN RECTORY,
CO. LONDONDERRY

107

108

110

109

111

112

117

116

113 114 115

THE DAIRY, BLAISE CASTLE, GLOUCESTERSHIRE

119

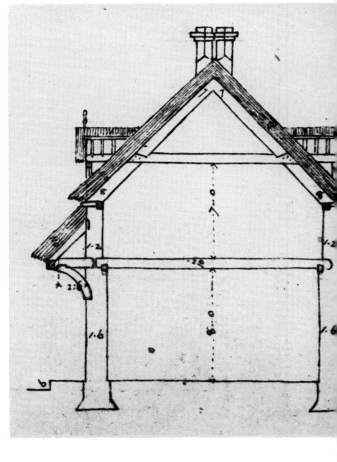

Mouldings
marked A

Top of Pier

Section of
the whole
of the
mould of
B

George make a fair drawing of this to ½ Scale
which is not figured to be taken by Scale

120   SKETCH FOR NEO-TUDOR LODGE

121
LODGE,
WHITSON COURT,
MONMOUTHSHIRE

122

LODGES, MOCCAS, HEREFORDSHIRE

123

124 ORNAMENTAL TOWER, CAERHAYES, CORNWALL

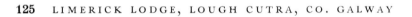

125 LIMERICK LODGE, LOUGH CUTRA, CO. GALWAY

126   DRUIDICAL TEMPLE FOR BLAISE CASTLE, GLOUCESTERSHIRE

Public Buildings

NASH'S CHRONOLOGICAL PROGRESS from the design of prisons to palaces was rapid. In 1795 he had completed his third and last gaol — at Hereford — and by 1812 he had found Royal favour and was starting to build a country palace to be known as the King's Cottage at Windsor.

Unless we count the Regent Street and Regent's Park developments as public buildings (which strictly they were not, as many private speculators were involved and the buildings were not public in the normal sense of the word) Nash left a small legacy in this category. Seven churches, four bridges, two hospitals, two monuments, two theatres, one institution, one market house and one town hall was its extent. As a list, this may sound impressive but in fact Nash's concern with these buildings was superficial and in most cases merely entailed small additions, reconstructions or alterations. The majority of this work was, in any case, done early in his career and acted as a springboard to greater things.

His least successful undertakings were his bridges and churches. None of the bridges survived and three of them collapsed after a short time. His two London churches were bitterly criticised and All Souls', Langham Place, has only become properly appreciated within the last few years.

Had Nash not elected to share the unpopularity of an extravagant monarch he might well have found favour with those responsible for public building schemes — for it was only the King's personal caprices that ultimately led to his disgrace. He was more successful when he concerned himself with such ventures as his insular work in the Isle of Wight — far away from a resentful Government.

GUILDHALL, Newport, Isle of Wight. 1814.

[127]. *A stuccoed composition with Ionic columns.*

Nash designed several public buildings on the Isle of Wight at the time he was building his own house there, one of which was the Guildhall. A disfiguring clock tower was added to the right of the portico in the late nineteenth century and all but ruins this plain scholarly composition.

Nash's original working drawings are preserved in the Borough Surveyor's office and the building cost £10,000.

ALL SOULS', Langham Place, London. 1822.

[128–131]. *A Classical composition in Bath stone closing the vista at the north end of Regent Street.*

Nash designed two churches in London, both entirely different in style and both much criticised by contemporary observers. All Souls' was the target of every form of lampoon, cartoon and public derision. It was, in fact, a brilliant solution to the problem of how to marry the north end of Regent Street to the south end of Portland Place further to the northwest. The round steeple and portico form the perfect link, and the main body of the church is cunningly tucked away, unseen from the main vistas. The effectiveness of its siting is seen in [172]. The fluted conical steeple encircled by a peristyle of Corinthian columns is unique and, although it was the main cause for censure, is an ingenious architectural feature. The capitals of the portico [129] are of an elaborate Ionic order made of Coade's pale terra-cotta and contain unusual cherubs' heads between the volutes based on a design by Michelangelo. The balustrade on the parapet of the main building, matching that of the portico, has long been removed and from certain angles the great slate roof is insufficiently concealed. [130] shows the plan and west elevation drawn by Pugin for Britton's *Edifices of London*, 1828. Britton, one of Nash's few champions for All Souls', states that the contract price was £15,994 and this figure was very little exceeded.

The interior follows the familiar pattern of Classical churches of the period. A gallery runs round three sides and simulated yellow marble columns rise from gallery level to cornice. The ceiling is coffered and is richly embellished with plaster mouldings and large rosettes. The marble font, organ case and Communion balusters (re-adapted) are all relics of Nash's original fittings.

The church was severely damaged during the Second World War, when a bomb pierced the roof, destroying the interior and removing the top of the spire. Extensive restoration work was carried out after the War by H. S. Goodhart-Rendel and the church was re-dedicated by the Bishop of London on 29 April 1951.

ST MARY'S, Haggerston, London. 1826.

[132]. *A Gothic church with tall tower built of Bath stone by John Walters.*

This strange church was built from designs provided by Nash and it was severely criticised at the time. It was certainly an eccentric pile and had great areas of undecorated wall-space, the tower itself being particularly stark. The lantern at its summit, however, surrounded by elaborate finials, was arresting. Smaller polygonal twin towers flanked the main tower and were surmounted by stone domes. Even by 1908 the church's critics were no less harsh and it was described as 'the bathos of Gothic burlesque . . . designed by Nash, the perpetrator of another absurdity in quite a different quarter of the town, viz. the steeple of All Souls', Langham Place'.

The original estimate for building was £12,998 but this sum was actually under-cut by £18.

A plaque bearing the following inscription is fixed to the drinking-fountain in the church-yard: 'On this site stood St Mary's parish church of Haggerston, destroyed by enemy action, 16 October 1940.'

ST DAVID'S CATHEDRAL, Pembroke-shire. 1791.

[133, 134]. *The re-building of the west front.*

The west front of the Norman cathedral had been raised on marshland and had been a source of trouble since 1180. The wall, under the great pressure of the Norman arcade, overhung its base by over twelve inches. It was Nash's job to correct this and to design a completely new west front. It was a highly complicated undertaking, Nash himself making these meticulous drawings of the work to be carried out. The result, although it stopped the west front from leaning further, was a crude mixture of buttresses, turrets and other clumsy features. The design was never admired at the time and survived only until 1862 when it was replaced with an imitation of the original Norman front by Sir George Gilbert Scott, who also completely restored the Cathedral.

152–154 ALBANY STREET, London. 1818.

[135]. *An unorthodox building in the Greek taste with central cupola.*

Nash built this composition on land leased to himself and it was the most interesting building in Albany Street. It was designed as an ophthalmic hospital for soldiers blinded in the Egyptian campaigns and later was used consecutively as a workshop, factory and market. The façade was impressive and bore no relation to the perfunctory premises behind.

The left-hand section, including the cupola, still exists but the remainder has been destroyed and a filling station (wittily named 'Nash's Sales and Service') now occupies the site.

ABERYSTWYTH BRIDGE, Cardigan-shire. c. 1800.

[136]. *A stone bridge over the Rheidol.*

Nash apparently supervised some of the work on this bridge but as it was not completed until after his return to London and his fees amounted to only £10. 18s. 6d., we can take it that Nash's interest in the project was limited. A gale swept away the bridge in 1886.

HEREFORD GAOL. 1795.

[137]. *A rugged stone building in Classical style.*

Of the three gaols Nash designed, Hereford was perhaps the most interesting and certainly the most impressive. It was designed to serve as a county gaol and 'house of correction'. It consisted of four galleried wings joined to a square hall with splayed angles. The central feature of the main elevation was an odd composition of Doric columns draped with real chains and partly decorated with vermiculations.

The building, for which Nash was paid £720 and his travelling expenses, was demolished in 1928.

THE ISLE OF WIGHT INSTITUTION, Newport. 1811.

[138]. *A stone building with pilasters and pediment.*

The Institution was built by local subscription and cost £3,000. Now known as The County Club, it has been little altered and represents Nash at his most disciplined.

The capitals have been renewed and a clothing store now occupies part of the ground floor.

THEATRE ROYAL, Haymarket, London. 1821.

[139]. *A stucco composition closing the vista along Charles II Street from St. James's Square.*

The exterior of the theatre with its massive Corinthian portico extending over the pavement has changed little since it was first built. The only alterations are the insertion of a round window in the pediment and disfiguring red paint carried some way up the columns. The interior contained some handsome detail of the period including columns in the form of palm trees to support the proscenium and the decorations were carried out in gold, pink and crimson.

The interior has twice been remodelled and nothing remains of the original fittings.

BRIDGE AND PAGODA, ST JAMES'S PARK, London. 1814.

[140]. *Part of the decorations for a firework display.*

The bridge and pagoda were erected for the centenary celebrations of the accession of George I, held on 1 August 1814 and formed the central feature of the display. Rockets, squibs and silvery showers issued from every floor of the pagoda but at midnight disaster occurred. The pagoda suddenly caught fire and fell into the lake, killing two men.

The bridge, although never much admired at the time, survived until 1820 when Nash was commissioned to replace it with an iron one.

128

HEREFORD GAOL

137

138 ISLE OF WIGHT INSTITUTION, NEWPORT

139 THEATRE ROYAL, HAYMARKET, LONDON

140 BRIDGE AND PAGODA, ST JAMES'S PARK, LONDON

Palaces, Town Houses

and Metropolitan Developments

NASH'S SCHEME for Regent Street, outlined on page 15, formed only a part of his great plan for the development of London. Another important aspect was the transformation of Marylebone Park, then isolated farm-land north of Portland Place, into one of the most splendid architectural panoramas in Europe.

London's streets and squares already contained mansions of considerable grandeur but the plan for Regent's Park was to offer something different — something unique. The snobbery of living in a terrace that looked like a great mansion was no novelty. Georgian terraces had already provided this illusion — individual houses sharing common pediments, porticoes, columns and other unifying features. But to live in a vast plaster palace overlooking what appeared to be boundless private park-land filled with rare trees, undulating lawns and sparkling lakes was irresistible.

As with the Regent Street buildings, we must appreciate Nash's terraces in the Park as a whole — as an attempt to provide the most enticing residential area ever conceived for a capital city and, whatever faults we find in the individual compositions, the lay-out we see today is a monument to the only man in the history of British architecture who managed to get such an ambitious town-planning scheme off the drawing-board and into reality.

In 1828 James Elmes, himself an architect and the author of a life of Sir Christopher Wren, wrote *Metropolitan Improvements or London in the Nineteenth Century*. [142] shows the title page of the book which is a remarkable record of the likes and dislikes of a discerning critic of the day. It contains a series of dramatic engravings from drawings by Thomas Shepherd and the text describes the new architectural wonders on the London scene. Elmes found it difficult to ignore Nash's lack of respect for the proper use of Classical elements and his disregard of what he called 'pure style' in some of the Regent's Park and Regent Street buildings. We must commend him for saying so in a book which he humbly dedicated

to the King who was, after all, Nash's devoted patron.

Nash received many other Royal commissions whilst under the patronage of the King, whose growing discontent with his only London residence — Carlton House — eventually ended the architect's career. Nash decorated the low-ceilinged rooms of Carlton House (or Carlton Palace as it was sometimes known) in styles of great magnificence but the results were short-lived and he spent the last active years of his career on the ill-fated hazard of re-building Buckingham House.

CUMBERLAND TERRACE, London. 1826.

[141, 153–155]. *A range of houses on the east side of the Park with great central pediment supported by ten Ionic columns.*

The terrace comprises five main blocks of houses divided by decorative arches behind which are set pairs of smaller houses. These sub-divisions and recesses save the terrace from monotony and seen as a whole the effect is impressive and must rank as Nash's most spectacular single composition. The pediment is filled with sculpture by J. G. Bubb representing Britannia surrounded by the various arts and sciences. Close examination shows the sculpture to be perfunctory and naïve but it is sufficiently decorative when seen from afar. The scale of the tower block seen in [155] is spoiled by a Victorian fourth storey addition. The interiors of the houses are spacious but have dull cantilever staircases. The drawing-room floors are of the usual good proportions with cornices of the period, fluted door architraves and white marble chimney-pieces.

Since the Second World War the houses have been used as Government offices but part of the terrace is under reconstruction as flats and the remainder will be retained as whole houses.

PARK CRESCENT, London. 1812.

[143,144]. *A crescent of twenty-nine houses forming an entrance to Regent's Park from the south.*

Originally designed as a circus, Park Crescent would have been the largest circle of buildings in Europe, but in its completed form, open to Regent's Park on the north, it is still Nash's most successful piece of domestic terrace architecture, providing a link between the country-like appearance of the Park and the sophisticated street architecture to the south. It is, however, surprising that Nash did not attempt to soften the rather abrupt joining of these great stucco terraces to the Georgian façades of Portland Place (which he considered to be the finest street in London) by the use of brick from first-floor level. None the less, the effect of the great curves of Ionic colonnades stretching outwards to the greenery of the Park is in itself unrivalled and forms the perfect introduction to the architectural scenes beyond.

The interiors of the houses were planned and detailed to the requirements and tastes of individual tenants, and several contain fine oval cantilevered staircases with domes. The cast ironwork round the Crescent gardens is especially good [144] and was probably designed by Nash. The obelisks no longer support lamps (see end-papers) and some of the ironwork has been removed. The disfiguring fourth-storey additions seen in [143] are soon to be removed.

The crescent was severely bombed in the Second World War and there are plans to demolish the remaining houses in the west quadrant, reconstructing the façade to screen modern buildings.

GLOUCESTER GATE, London. 1827.

[145]. *A terrace of eleven houses, with several detached houses adjoining, at the most northerly point of the Park.*

The terrace was built by R. Mott, the façade designed by Nash and the work carried out by Mott's architect John Joseph Scoles. Scoles did not like Nash's façade and tried to alter it by enlarging the cornice. This had the result of dwarfing the Ionic pilasters and columns below, but Nash merely remarked when he saw it that 'the parts looks larger than expected'. To the untutored eye, however, the building is imposing and the interiors of the houses are on a more generous scale than those in some of the other terraces.

The houses are occupied privately.

ULSTER TERRACE, London. 1824.

[146]. *One of a pair of terraces facing the Park set at right angles to Park Square West.*

These houses make up one of the few terraces not disguised as a palace. They are very clearly individual houses with remarkably generous bow windows to the end houses rising the whole height of the building. An Ionic order is used on the ground floor carrying through the Ionic themes of Park Crescent and Park Square West seen on the left. The rooms in the houses with bow windows are pleasant, but the terrace has suffered more than any other from ugly additions to the upper storeys. The twin terrace lies east of Park Square and is called St Andrew's Place, a cul-de-sac containing a Corinthian porticoed building by George Thompson comprising two houses. On the right in the engraving can be seen an Ionic composition which was completely destroyed during the Second World War.

PARK SQUARE EAST, London. 1823–25.

[147, 148]. *One of a pair of Ionic terraces on the south side of the Park.*

The terraces, Park Square East and West, were designed to enjoy the gardens they face, laid out by Nash in place of the abandoned scheme for Park Crescent to be a vast circus. The centre of the east terrace was designed as a 'Diorama' by Pugin. The interior contained a revolving salon and spectators were shown first one and then another scene projected on to a screen in 'magic lantern' style. This portion of the terrace is now used as a clinic. The tops of the round-arched windows are false and do not light the rooms within.

The terraces, although quite impressive, seem cramped after the spacious and dramatic planning of Park Crescent, but because of their moderate size the houses are still occupied privately as single units.

SUSSEX PLACE, London. 1822.

[149–152]. *A terrace of twenty-six houses on the west side of the Park.*

This composition was undoubtedly intended to be seen from a distance, now made impossible by the height of the trees in the gardens and the Park. It is a mildly exotic design of curved wings, semi-hexagonal bays and ten steep, pointed domes, strung together with balustrades and fifty-six Corinthian columns. Although much criticised when built, its capricious qualities are acceptable and endearing today.

The spacious gardens in front of the terrace are beautifully planted and provide spectacular panoramic views from the houses in the curved wings. As in many of the terraces, most of the original glazing bars have been replaced by plate glass, depriving the building of an important feature. The houses with bays have pretty oval cantilevered staircases rising the whole height of the house [149], and some contain good marble fireplaces ([152] shows one in the drawing-room of No. 20). The internal cornices and other Classical details are refined and well considered.

The building may later be reconstructed as flats.

YORK TERRACE, London. 1822.

[157]. *A bipartite building on the south side of the Park flanking York Gate.*

In these immensely long ranges of houses, Nash used a Greek Ionic order, a departure from his usual Roman. The terrace is a splendid example of Nash's success when designing for panoramic scenic effect. The composition comprises two great 'palaces' containing forty-nine houses of similar accommodation. The ground floor is rusticated and a Greek Doric colonnade joins the end blocks to the pedimented centre block. The houses are entered from a lane at the rear and although the entrance halls and staircases are less mean than in some of the other terraces, the interiors are not of great interest. Also numbered in York Terrace is a pair of houses known as Doric Villa [156].

At present mostly used as Government offices, the terrace is to be converted into flats.

YORK GATE, London. 1819.

[158, 159]. *Twin terraces forming a vista to Hardwick's parish church and an entrance to the Park from the south.*

Elmes considered York Gate to be a successful piece of architecture (although he made a few reservations about the details) and it certainly remains today one of the few examples of spacious town-planning. Seen from the church, the terracs form a clear-cut and imposing entrance to the greenery beyond and frame the church well when looking from the Park. The façades are of a plain Ionic order and the end houses have Doric porches.

The terraces are at present used as Government offices and were restored after damage in the Second World War.

CORNWALL TERRACE, London. 1821.

[160–163]. *A terrace of nineteen houses, on the south side of the Park.*

Decimus Burton, who was responsible for several villas and other buildings in the Park, probably designed this terrace under Nash's wing. The largest house in the centre has a portico with six great free-standing columns and the house on the extreme west end has a handsome bow window decorated with caryatids [161]. (Also seen in [162], a fine sepia drawing in the Crace Collection, British Museum.) A modern addition to this bow and an unsuitable wrought-iron canopy to the front door have robbed this part of the building of its elegance. The cast-iron lamp standards in the terrace are original and very fine [160]. This is one of the few buildings without gardens between the façade and the Park.

The terrace is at present used as Government offices.

CHESTER TERRACE, London. 1825.

[164, 165]. *The longest unbroken terrace in the Park, on the east side.*

The houses in this terrace are smaller than those in Cumberland Terrace and the scheme is less ambitious and full of careless detail. The three Corinthian porticoes appear heavy and gauche grouped along the vast façade of the terrace. The great 'triumphal' arches, set at right-angles to each end, merely serve as thin theatrical screens to the composition.

The interiors of the houses are dull with narrow entrance halls, but the terrace as a whole, however ungrammatical, has an expansive air and the houses enjoy fine views of gardens and Park.

The terrace is shortly to be developed as flats.

HANOVER TERRACE, London. 1822.

[166, 167]. *A terrace of twenty houses on the west side of the Park with three Roman Doric porticoes.*

This is one of the more scholarly of the terraces and the general effect is one of grandeur and rich detail.

The continuous segmental arches are pleasing although making the ground floor rooms dark. The pediments are filled with decorative sculpture of a clear-cut and effective design, and Classical figures flank the pediments and form finials to the apexes. The interiors are not interesting, with dull staircases and long, narrow entrance halls. The ironwork is all good of its type, but has been removed from the gardens in front of the terrace. The houses have splendid views of the lake and Park beyond, and are to be retained as private houses.

SOMERIES HOUSE, London. 1824.

[168]. *A plain square stuccoed house set at an angle to the road between Cambridge Gate and St Andrew's Place.*

This is the only detached house in Regent's Park designed by Nash. It was originally the Adult Orphan Asylum and he gave his services free in order that the cost of building should be minimised.

The house later became a private residence, was much enlarged, is now used as Government offices and is soon to be demolished to make way for a modern building.

115 REGENT STREET, London. 1824.

[169, 170]. *A domed building on the corner of Vigo Street.*

This was one of Nash's clever methods of terminating a long terrace of shops on the corner of a street. The building was also an important feature in the vista formed by the

Quadrant [178]. The fluted Corinthian pilasters and strong cornices gave the composition a handsome and substantial look. [169 — a photograph taken in 1898] shows No. 115 as being one of the few façades that had not been mutilated and altered by that date.

232 REGENT STREET, London. c. 1824.

[171, 172]. *A clumsy composition in neo-Greek taste.*

This island site formed part of the east side of Regent Street and the projecting pavilions had free-standing Ionic columns two storeys in height. These pavilions were surmounted at each corner by acroters each containing an anthemion and the windows were flanked by ugly vase-shaped columns. By 1898 [171] this grotesque composition had not been improved by the addition of another floor, pretentious fascia boards and undisciplined shop windows.

242–4 REGENT STREET, London. 1822.

[173]. *A pavilion with balustraded bow of the Corinthian order.*

This composition is another example of Nash's way of terminating a block on a corner site and its bowed front would have made an impressive feature in the street when viewed from a distance. The shop-front, seen in this 1898 photograph, is one of the less dissonant alterations that were made to the Regent Street buildings during the last half of the nineteenth century.

246 REGENT STREET, London. 1819.

[174]. *A plain building on the east side of the street with a balcony supported on termini surmounted by female heads.*

This curious composition was known as the Harmonic Institute — a concert hall — and the premises also included a music shop. Elmes stated that the broad portico made the ground-floor rooms unpleasantly dark but admitted that the termini provided a pleasing variety in the street. Bubb, who also produced the sculpture for the pediment of Cumberland Terrace [141], modelled the heads. The interior was lavish and contained a ball-room hung with crimson flock paper figured in gold and lit by three chandeliers, a drawing-room, an ante-room (both hung with green flock paper) and a grand concert hall. Spohr, Weber and Mendelssohn performed in this building which was then the centre of fashionable musical circles. It was burnt down in 1830 and rebuilt without the portico. On the right can be seen the portico of Hanover Chapel (1825) by Charles Robert Cockerell.

171–95 REGENT STREET, London. 1822.

[175]. *A great composition of shops and offices on the west side of the street decorated with Corinthian pilasters.*

Built by Burton to Nash's designs, this was one of the most spectacular buildings in the street and its pilasters, reaching from the pavement to the cornice, gave a rich and splendid impression. It was not long, however, before the building was mutilated and individual shop-keepers were allowed to cover up and cut into the pilasters at ground floor level, destroying the uniformity on which the composition depended for its effect.

THE COUNTY FIRE OFFICE, London. 1819.

[176, 177]. *An arcaded composition of the Corinthian order closing the vista looking from Waterloo Place along Lower Regent Street.*

The founder of The County Fire and Provident Life Insurance Office employed Robert Abraham as his architect but it is likely that Nash would have taken a keen interest in a building occupying this immensely important site. The street elevation resembled the south front of Inigo Jones's old Somerset House, a design with which Nash would have been quite familiar and he is almost certain to have at least indicated the design of the façade.

The present County Fire Office occupies the same site.

THE QUADRANT, Regent Street, London. 1818.

[178]. *A full quarter-circle composition with massive Doric colonnades leading from Piccadilly Circus.*

This was undoubtedly Nash's greatest set-piece in Regent Street and was the largest single composition. The impact of the vast sweeping colonnades was striking and Elmes, often a severe critic, described it as 'worthy of a Roman amphitheatre'. Viewed from the east side of the street the curve of the colonnades appeared to vanish into infinity and provided a splendid architectural scene on the grand scale. The columns were of cast iron on granite bases and the remainder of the façade was stuccoed. The colonnade was demolished in 1848.

The Quadrant was also one of Nash's personal speculations and he took over the whole site in order that the composition should develop as one unit rather than allowing individual buildings to spoil the continuous curve.

PICCADILLY CIRCUS, London. 1820.

[179]. *A circle of plain pilastered buildings forming a pivot between the northern and southern parts of Regent Street.*

The Quadrant was terminated by the County Fire

Office on the north [177] and by a tower-like pavilion on the south. In the Circus, broad shop windows were flanked by Ionic columns and the first and second floors were decorated with shallow, grooved pilasters. The pavilion at the end of the Quadrant contained a first-floor window with radial-fluted tympanum and a shop front with a pediment. The attic windows were oblong — a device Nash was fond of using. The plan of the Circus was considerably smaller than the shapeless arrangement we see in its place today.

29 DOVER STREET, London. *c.* 1800.

[180 and Plan 14]. *Nash's own Classical residence and office.*

This shows Nash's determination to outdo all other styles of domestic street architecture then building in London. The stuccoed façade contained many favourite tricks which he used in other designs. The coupled Ionic columns were later used at Park Crescent, and the oval windows had already been used at Llysnewydd and Southgate, and were to be used again later at Carlton House Terrace [66, 29, 187]. Inside, the house was spacious and well-planned. On the first floor was a drawing-room with adjoining domed alcove and a large library at the back with four Corinthian columns on pedestals. The second floor contained the drawing office where the Regent's Park and Regent Street plans were made.

The house was mutilated in 1934, bombed in 1941 and has since been entirely rebuilt.

SUFFOLK STREET, London. 1820.

[181]. *A narrow street of stuccoed buildings leading from Pall Mall.*

Several of the houses in this street remain as originally built, although Nash's Ionic composition seen on the right has vanished. The building belonging to the Royal Society of British Artists with its Doric portico survives. It was designed by Nash and Elmes (the architect and critic who founded the Society) and contains a gallery built over vaults which Nash, as leaseholder, let to great personal advantage.

SUFFOLK PLACE, HAYMARKET, London. 1820.

[182]. *A stuccoed composition on the corner of the Haymarket, leading to Suffolk Street.*

This is one of the very few remaining examples of Nash's London street planning. The first-floor windows contain his favourite tympanum device with elaborate shell motif and the cast ironwork is particularly good.

The building has recently been sympathetically restored by the American Express Company and may now be ap-preciated as an historic relic of the style and scale of London's Regency architecture.

CLARENCE HOUSE, London. 1825.

[184]. *A stuccoed house built for the Duke of Clarence adjoining St James's Palace.*

Little remains of the original façade which has been enlarged and altered over the years. Nash's building was of three main storeys and an attic storey. The section to the right of the bay windows was added in 1875 bringing it adjacent to the State apartments of St James's Palace. A full third floor, replacing an attic storey, was added at this time together with the bay windows and a conservatory over the porch seen in this late nineteenth-century engraving.

A few of the original ceilings, fireplaces and other details exist but the interior has largely been remodelled.

The house was in disrepair before the Second World War and later damaged by bombs. The building was then entirely reconstructed and re-planned as a London residence for Her Majesty the Queen, then H.R.H. Princess Elizabeth. It is now the London residence of Queen Elizabeth the Queen Mother and H.R.H. Princess Margaret.

THE UNITED SERVICE CLUB, London. 1827.

[185, 186]. *A four-square stuccoed building on the corner of Waterloo Place and Pall Mall.*

The club-house is built on part of the site of Carlton House and the ground was leased by the Crown to the members at £600 per annum. Nash's original exterior was plain with coupled Doric columns forming porticoes on the south and west fronts, the north (entrance) front in Pall Mall having a pedimented upper portico of the Corinthian order. In 1858 Decimus Burton added pretentious decorations to the façades including an elaborate frieze below the cornice, possibly to compete with the Parthenon frieze he used in his design for the Athenæum Club on the opposite corner of Waterloo Place. He also substituted a stone balustrade for the cast-iron railings, removed the west portico, and extended the building east along Pall Mall.

The plan is arranged round a vast, square, double-return staircase lit by a square dome above a deep, coffered cove. Burton removed the coffering and substituted elaborate plasterwork. All the main rooms are monumental in scale, Classical in detail, and all have deep coves above dentilled cornices. The library on the first floor has two pairs of 'green marble' scagiola columns surmounted by gilt Corinthian capitals. The original white marble chimney-pieces are very fine and unusual gilt wood curtain rods of the period survive here and elsewhere in the club. The smoking-room under the library on the ground floor is similarly divided by columns, this time of 'yellow marble' scagiola of the Ionic order. Three massive gilt chandeliers in this room are probably original fittings. If Burton's alterations did nothing for the exterior, at least he installed attractive marble floors on the ground floor and replaced Nash's shoddy deal doors.

The building was severely damaged during the Second World War, since when it has been well restored.

CARLTON HOUSE TERRACE, London. 1827.

[187]. *A pair of Corinthian stuccoed terraces on the north side of The Mall facing St James's Park.*

These terraces took over five years to build and James Pennethorne supervised the construction of Nash's designs. They were part of a much larger scheme including terraces on the south side of The Mall which were never built. Nash wanted to put up a covered fountain between the terraces to form a feature when looking from Waterloo Place to the Park, but his critics in the Government were suspicious of his competence by then and asked whether the effect would be good. 'I hope so . . .' said Nash but when asked if he had ever seen a fountain in the form of a covered temple he had to admit that he had not, and the project was dropped.

The terraces are similar in conception to the blocks then being built in Regent's Park, but the houses are considerably larger and were more spaciously planned. The main façades are monumental in scale and impressive with their rows of giant Corinthian columns stretching the whole length of the composition. The tall end pavilions were probably introduced in order to provide some houses of greater accommodation than in the centre blocks. The houses were immediately taken by illustrious tenants and the terrace became the most fashionable address in London.

The buildings are now mostly occupied as Government offices and a large block of modern offices, inappropriate in style and scale, has been added to the north side of the west terrace.

CARLTON HOUSE, London. 1814.

[188]. *A Gothic dining-room forming part of a suite of magnificent State rooms for the Prince Regent.*

Pyne's *Royal Residences* (1819) illustrates a splendid series of rooms on the ground floor of Carlton House, the Prince Regent's only London house at the time. The rooms show Nash to be a highly competent interior decorator and all the trappings were of considerable richness, foretelling the even greater extravaganzas to follow at the Royal Pavilion. Most of the detail was Corinthian and the plasterwork was burnished with gold, and highly coloured.

The Gothic dining-room was the most interesting and curious of all the rooms. (This illustration is reproduced from an original drawing for Pyne's *Royal Residences* by gracious permission of H.M. The Queen.) Pairs of Gothic columns rose from fitted side-tables to support immense carved and pierced brackets from the ends of which hung eight cut-glass chandeliers. The windows had delicate Gothic glazing-bars and were festooned with silk draperies of contrasting colours. These elaborate decorations were wisely complemented by a perfectly plain ceiling and carpet. John Britton, on the other hand, wrote in 1828 that 'the flat ceiling produces a very bad effect, being quite incongruous to the style adopted; and this, in fact, is the less excusable, as it might have been vaulted, and rendered loftier, there being no apartments above it.' Britton also adds a note expressing his regret that the building was soon to be demolished and made a final plea for its portico to be rescued and used elsewhere. His plea was not quite in vain for some of the columns were re-used on the façade of the National Gallery.

Nash also devised several temporary rooms at Carlton House for various celebrations and festivities, but the place was never much liked by the Prince Regent who undoubtedly felt cramped in this low-ceilinged eighteenth-century house. It was demolished while Buckingham House was being transformed into the main royal residence and its site was covered by Carlton House Terrace, Carlton Gardens, and Waterloo Place. A distant view of the Ionic front can be seen at the south end of Regent Street in [179].

BUCKINGHAM PALACE, London. 1825.

[189–193]. *The enlargement of Buckingham House to form a London residence for George IV.*

Although Nash had produced suites of magnificent rooms in Carlton House, the King never liked living there and Buckingham House was suggested as an alternative. As we have seen on page 17, the rebuilding of Buckingham House was a sad, long-drawn-out affair and eventually led to the architect's downfall.

Much of Nash's work remains. The garden front, although somewhat altered, is consistent with Nash's design [189 and 191] and the Corinthian entrance portico is intact [192]. Nash himself sketched many of the elaborate mouldings and cornices and some of these sketches are preserved at The Victoria and Albert Museum. The interior has been constantly redecorated and remodelled and only one room, the Household Dining-room [193], remains much as Nash designed it.

The Marble Arch [190 and 194] has its own involved history. It was designed as the main triumphal entrance to the Palace and in fact formed a gateway set many yards away from the main forecourt, linked to it by iron railings. Nash sent to Italy for Ravaccione marble and the arch was duly erected as planned. The sculpture was provided by Westmacott, Baily and Chantrey. In 1847 it was dismantled and later reconstructed on its present site at the junction of Oxford Street and Park Lane and looks no more like marble today than do the monstrous modern blocks surrounding it.

METROPOLITAN IMPROVEMENTS;

OR

London,

in the

NINETEENTH CENTURY:

BEING A

SERIES OF VIEWS,

OF THE NEW AND MOST INTERESTING OBJECTS,

in the

BRITISH METROPOLIS & ITS VICINITY:

from Original Drawings by

Mr THOS. H. SHEPHERD.

WITH

HISTORICAL, TOPOGRAPHICAL & CRITICAL ILLUSTRATIONS,

BY

James Elmes, M.R.I.A.

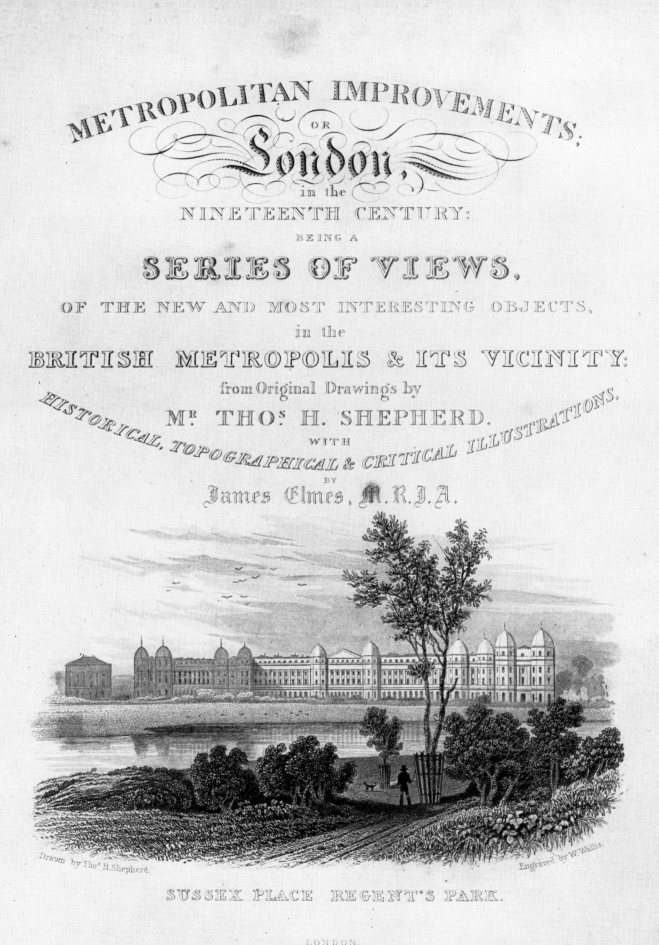

Drawn by Thos. H. Shepherd.

Engraved by W. Wallis.

SUSSEX PLACE REGENT'S PARK.

LONDON.

Published May 5, 1827, by Jones & Co. 3, Acton Place, Kingsland Road.

143 PARK CRESCENT, LONDON

145
GLOUCESTER GATE,
LONDON

147 ▶

PARK SQUARE EAST,
LONDON

148 ▶

ULSTER TERRACE, LONDON 146

150

◀ **149**   SUSSEX PLACE, LONDON

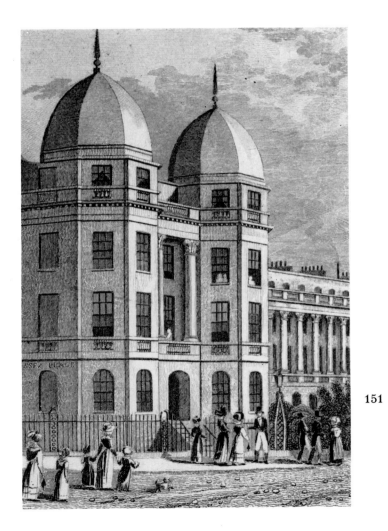

151

152

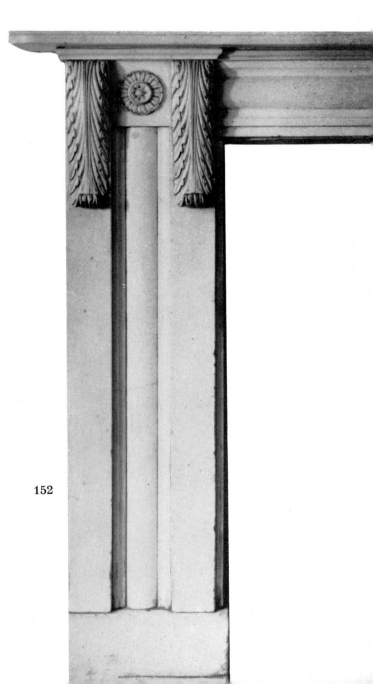

153

154

CUMBERLAND TERRACE, LONDON

156 DORIC VILLA, YORK TERRACE, LONDON

157 YORK TERRACE, LONDON

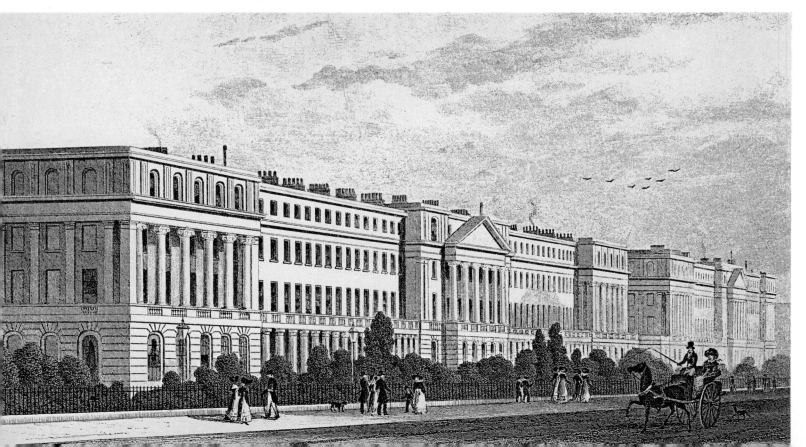

158

YORK GATE, LONDON

159

161

160

CORNWALL TERRACE, LONDON

162

174

REGENT STREET, LONDON

175

176   WATERLOO PLACE, LOWER REGENT STREET, LONDON

177   COUNTY FIRE OFFICE, REGENT STREET, LONDON ▶

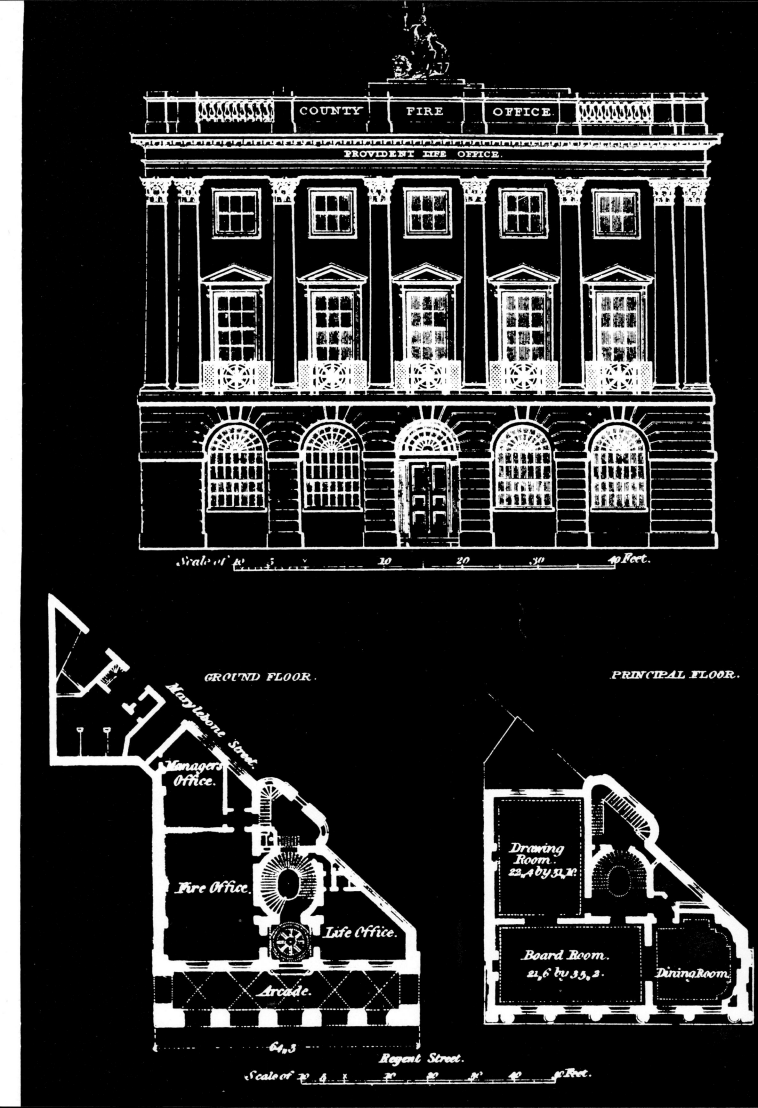

COUNTY FIRE OFFICE.

PROVIDENT LIFE OFFICE.

Scale of 10 5   10   20   30   40 Feet.

GROUND FLOOR.   PRINCIPAL FLOOR.

Marylebone Street.

Manager's
Office.

Fire Office.

Life Office.

Drawing
Room.
22,4 by 31,9.

Board Room.
21,6 by 35,2.

Dining Room.

Arcade.

64,3

Regent Street.

Scale of 10 5   10   20   30   40   50 Feet.

178   THE QUADRANT, REGENT STREET, LONDON

180   29, DOVER STREET, LONDON ▶

179   PICCADILLY CIRCUS, LONDON

181 SUFFOLK STREET, LONDON

182
SUFFOLK PLACE,
LONDON

183
BLOOMSBURY SQUARE,
LONDON

184 CLARENCE HOUSE,
LONDON

185

UNITED SERVICE CLUB, LONDON

186

187 CARLTON HOUSE TERRACE, LONDON

188 GOTHIC DINING ROOM, CARLTON HOUSE, LONDON

189

190

191

BUCKINGHAM PALACE, LONDON

192

193

Index of Buildings Illustrated

Aberystwyth, bridge [136]
Albany Street, Ophthalmic Hospital [135]
All Souls', Langham Place [128–131]
Aqualate Hall [43]
Attingham [37, 38]

Blaise [106–119, 126]
Bridge Lodge, Moccas [123]
Brighton, Royal Pavilion [1, 2]
Buckingham Palace [189–193]

Caerhayes Castle [63–65, 124]
Carlton House [188]
Carlton House Terrace [187]
Casina, Dulwich [57]
Chester Terrace [164, 165]
Childwall Hall [58]
Clarence House [184]
Cornwall Terrace [160–163]
County Fire Office [176, 177]
Cronkhill [15–17 and Plan 4]
Cumberland Terrace [141, 153–155]

Daw's Lodge, Moccas [122]
Dolaucothi [69, 70]
Doric Villa, York Terrace [156]
Dover Street, 29 [180 and Plan 14]

East Cowes Castle [39–42 and Plan 6]

Ffynone [49–54 and Plan 9]

Garnstone [27, 28]
Gloucester Gate [145]
Gracefield [98–102]
Guildhall, Newport, Isle of Wight [127]

Hanover Terrace [166, 167]
Hereford Gaol [137]

Isle of Wight Institution, Newport [138]

Kentchurch Court [45]
Killy Moon Castle [25, 26 and Plan 5]
Kilwaughter Castle [44 and Plan 7]
King's Cottage, Windsor [55]

Knepp Castle [72–74 and Plan 11]

Liphook, villa [91, 92]
Lissan Rectory [105 and Plan 13]
Llysnewydd [66–68 and Plan 10]
Longner Hall [85–89]
Lough Cutra Castle [81–84, 125]
Luscombe Castle [59–62]

Marble Arch [190, 194]
Marine Villa, Cowes [104]

Park Crescent [143, 144]
Park Square East [147, 148]
Park Village East [94, 95, 97]
Park Village West [90, 93, 96]
Point Pleasant, Kingston-on-Thames [103]

Ravensworth Castle [11–14]
Regent Street [169–179]
Rockingham [46, 47]

St David's Cathedral [133, 134]
St James's Park, bridge and pagoda [140]
St Mary's, Haggerston [132]
Sandridge Park [75–80 and Plan 12]
Shanbally Castle [18–24]
Sion House, Tenby [71]
Someries House [168]
Southborough Place [3–7 and Plan 3]
Southgate Grove [29–36]
Suffolk Place [182]
Suffolk Street [181]
Sussex Place [149–152]

Theatre Royal, Haymarket [139]

Ulster Terrace [146]
United Service Club [185, 186]

West Grinstead Park [8–10]
Whitson Court [48, 121 and Plan 8]
Witley Court [56]

York Gate [158, 159]
York Terrace [157]

Complete lists of known works are to be found in *A Biographical Dictionary of English Architects* by H. M. Colvin and *John Nash: architect to King George IV* by Sir John Summerson.

The lists contain information on works not illustrated in this book, such as designs for numerous lodges, gates, stabling and other improvements for country estates; projects that were not executed or are unidentified; undated works and buildings that have been demolished.

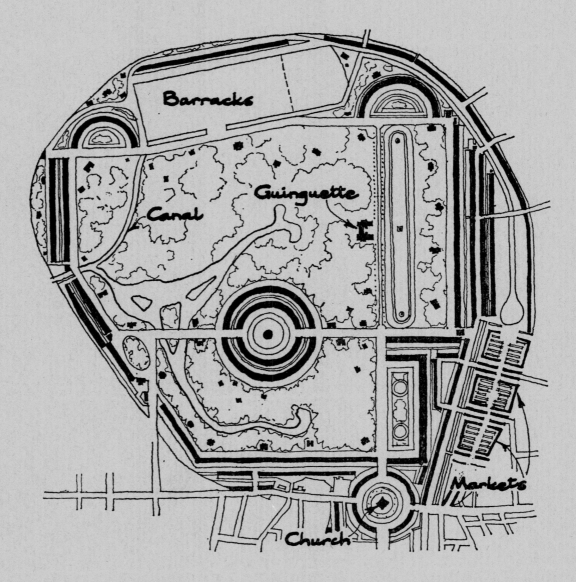

PLAN I — FIRST PLAN FOR REGENT'S PARK (1812). SEE PAGE 14

Key giving main London
works illustrated or
mentioned in the text

 I   REGENT'S CANAL
 2   GLOUCESTER GATE
 3   PARK VILLAGE EAST
 4   PARK VILLAGE WEST
 5   HANOVER TERRACE
 6   SUSSEX PLACE
 7   CUMBERLAND TERRACE
 8   CHESTER TERRACE
 9   CAMBRIDGE TERRACE
10   CORNWALL TERRACE
11   SOMERIES HOUSE
12   YORK TERRACE
13   YORK GATE
14   ULSTER TERRACE
15   ST ANDREW'S PLACE
16   PARK SQUARE EAST
17   PARK CRESCENT
18   PORTLAND PLACE
19   ALL SOULS', LANGHAM PLACE
20   OXFORD CIRCUS
21   REGENT STREET
22   DOVER STREET
23   THE QUADRANT
24   PICCADILLY CIRCUS
25   SUFFOLK PLACE
26   SUFFOLK STREET
27   UNITED SERVICE CLUB
28   CARLTON HOUSE TERRACE
29   THE MALL
30   CLARENCE HOUSE
31   THE MARBLE ARCH
32   BUCKINGHAM PALACE

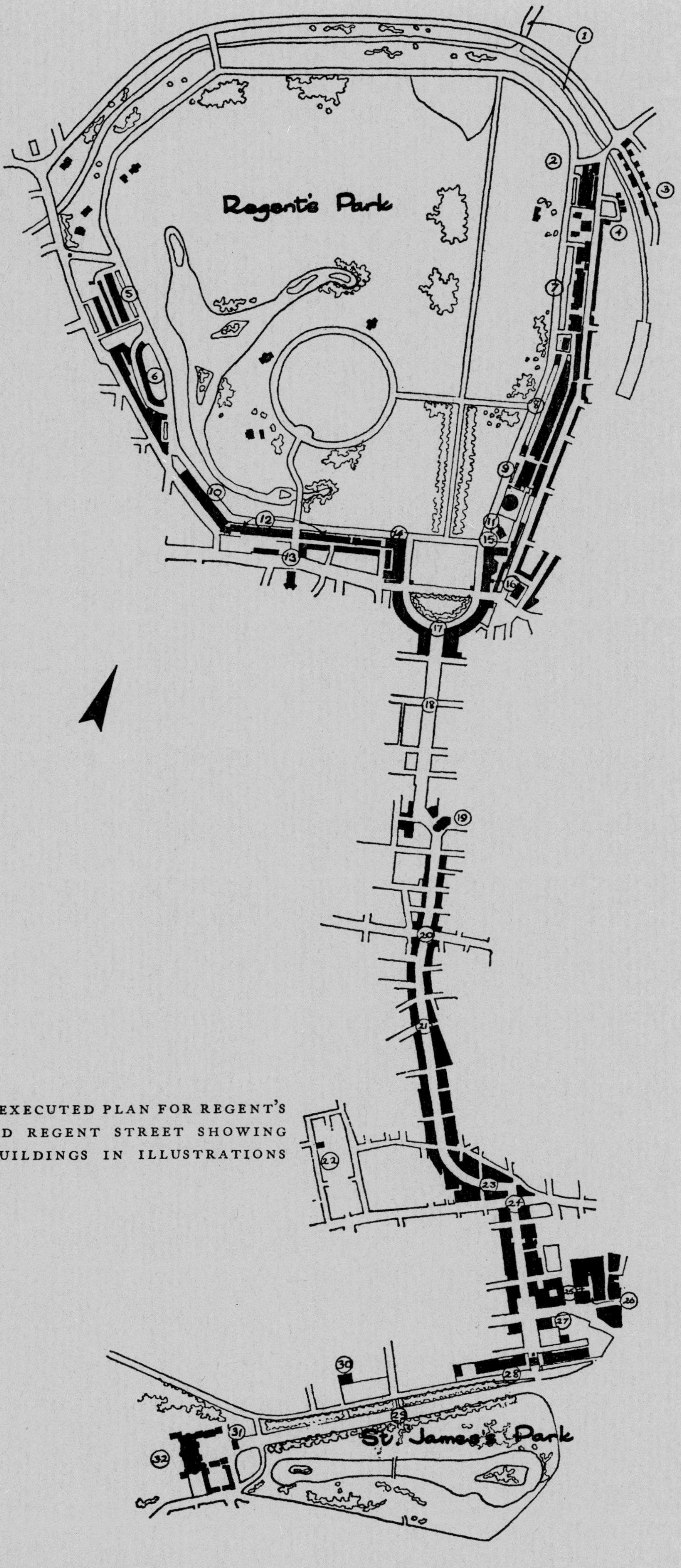

PLAN 2 — EXECUTED PLAN FOR REGENT'S
PARK AND REGENT STREET SHOWING
OTHER BUILDINGS IN ILLUSTRATIONS
[141–194]

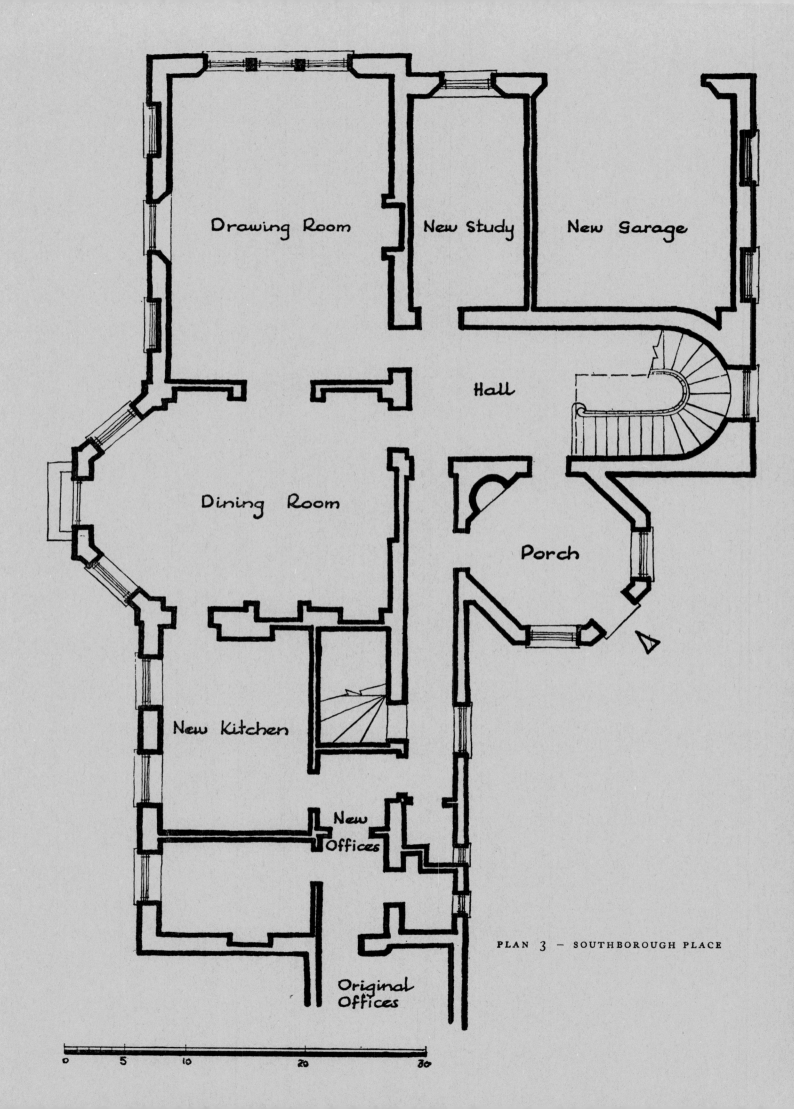

Drawing Room

New Study

New Garage

Hall

Dining Room

Porch

New Kitchen

New Offices

Original Offices

PLAN 3 — SOUTHBOROUGH PLACE

0   5   10   20   30

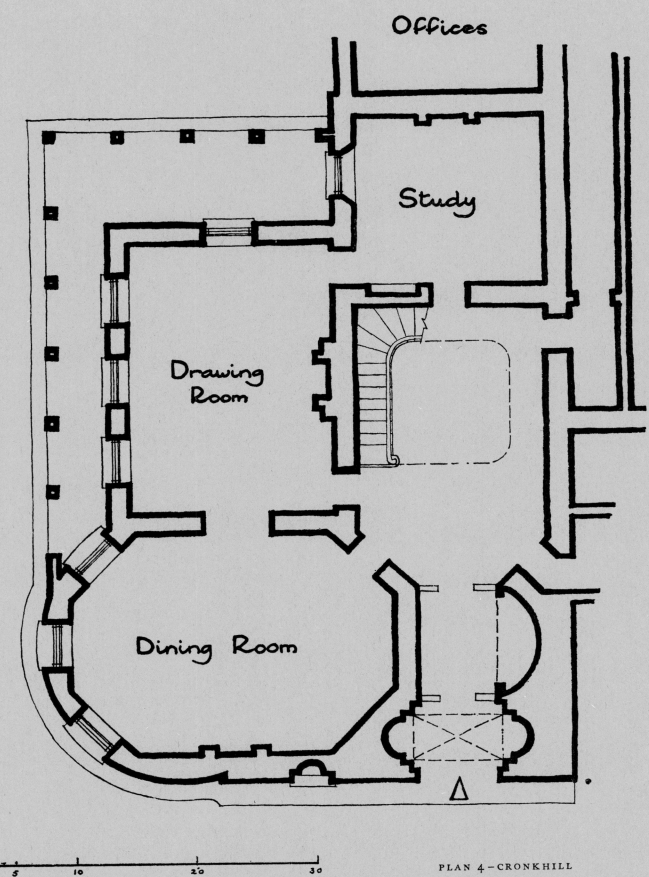

Offices

Study

Drawing
Room

Dining Room

0   5   10   20   30

PLAN 4—CRONKHILL

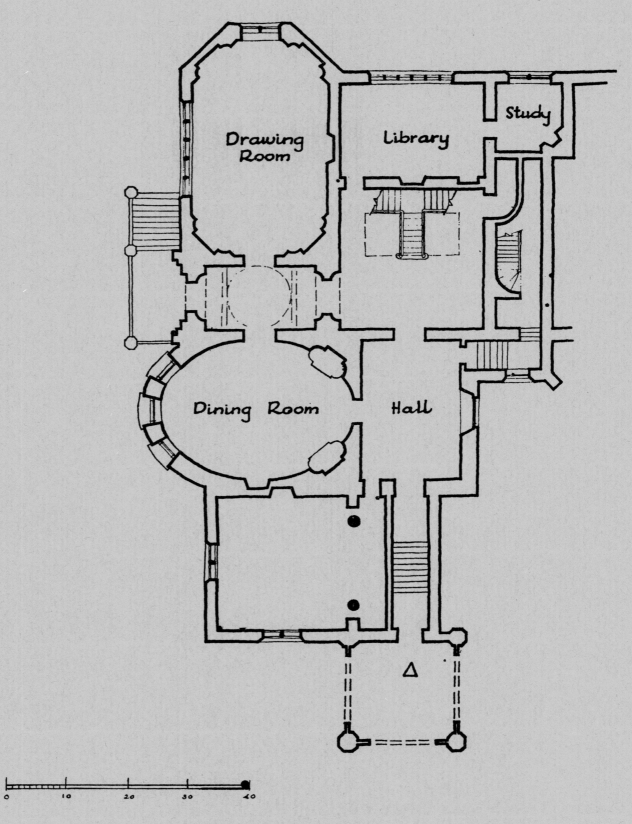

Drawing Room

Library

Study

Dining Room

Hall

0   10   20   30   40

PLAN 5 — KILLY MOON CASTLE

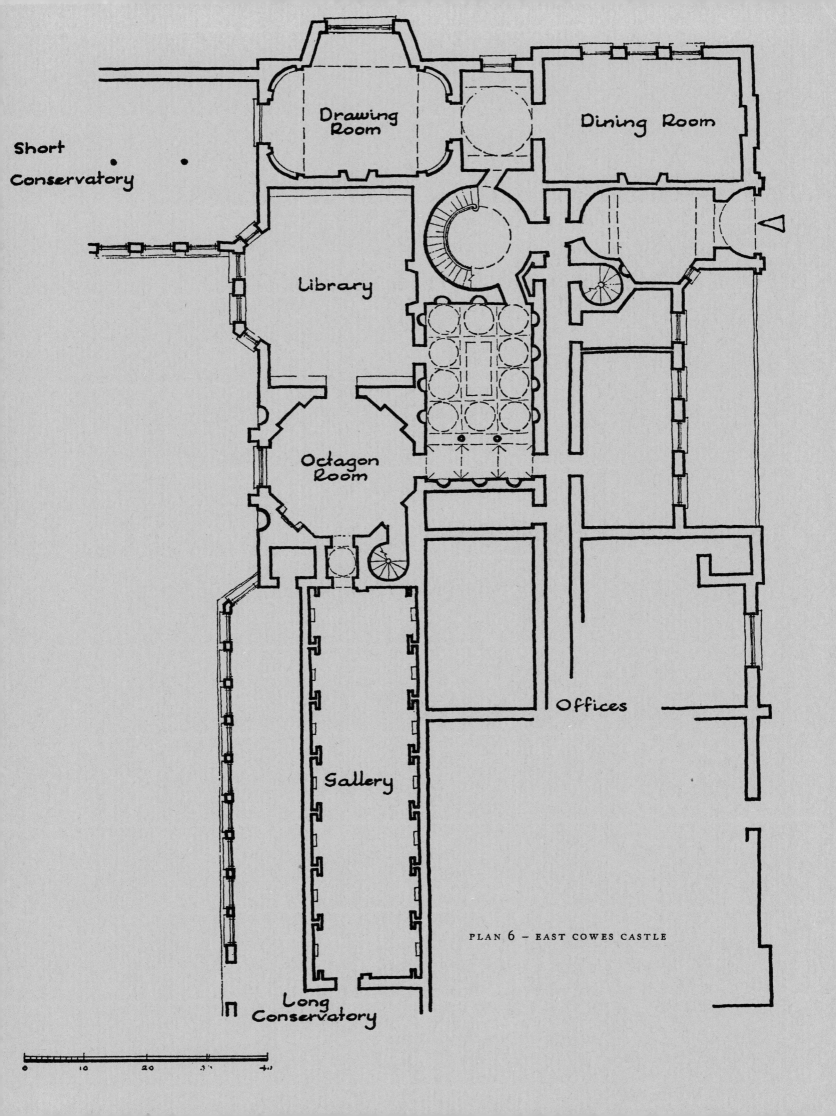

Short
Conservatory

Drawing
Room

Dining Room

Library

Octagon
Room

Gallery

Offices

PLAN 6 – EAST COWES CASTLE

Long
Conservatory

0   10   20   30   40

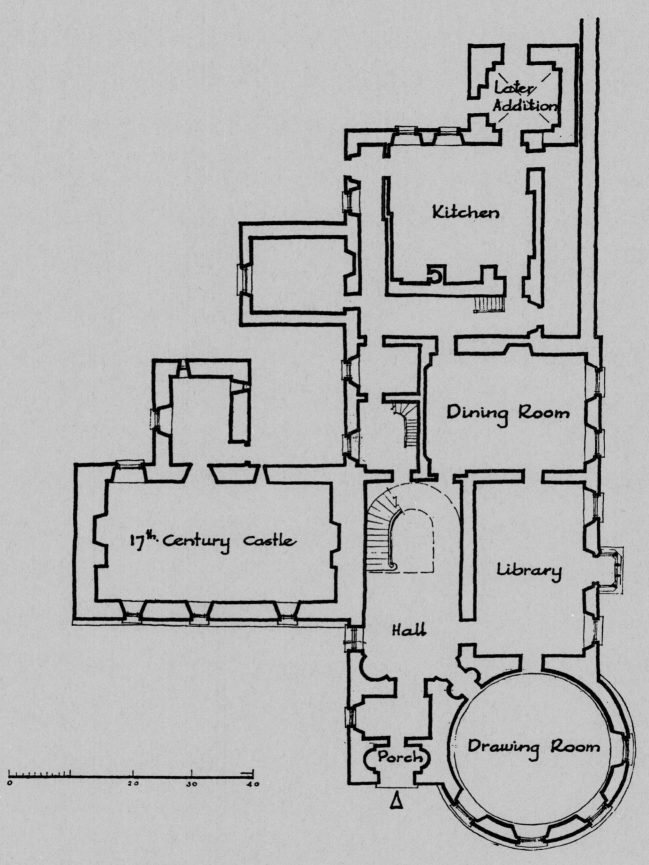

Later Addition

Kitchen

Dining Room

17ᵗʰ. Century Castle

Library

Hall

Porch

Drawing Room

0   20   30   40

PLAN 7 – KILWAUGHTER CASTLE

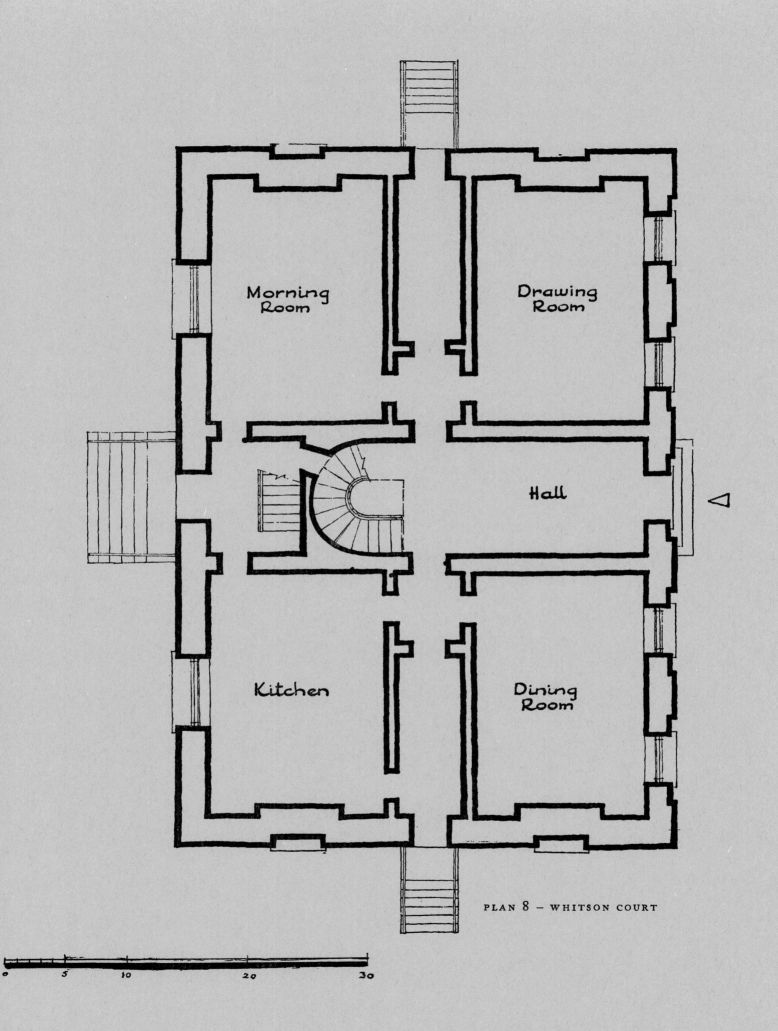

Morning
Room

Drawing
Room

Hall

Kitchen

Dining
Room

PLAN 8 — WHITSON COURT

0   5   10   20   30

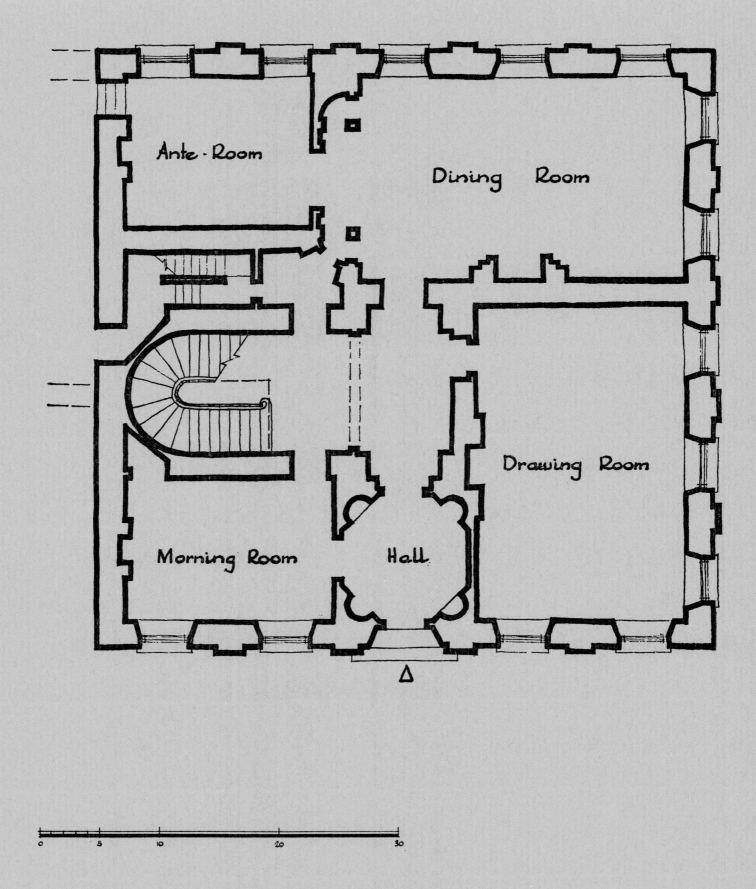

Ante · Room

Dining   Room

Drawing Room

Morning Room

Hall

Δ

0   5   10   20   30

PLAN 9 — FFYNONE

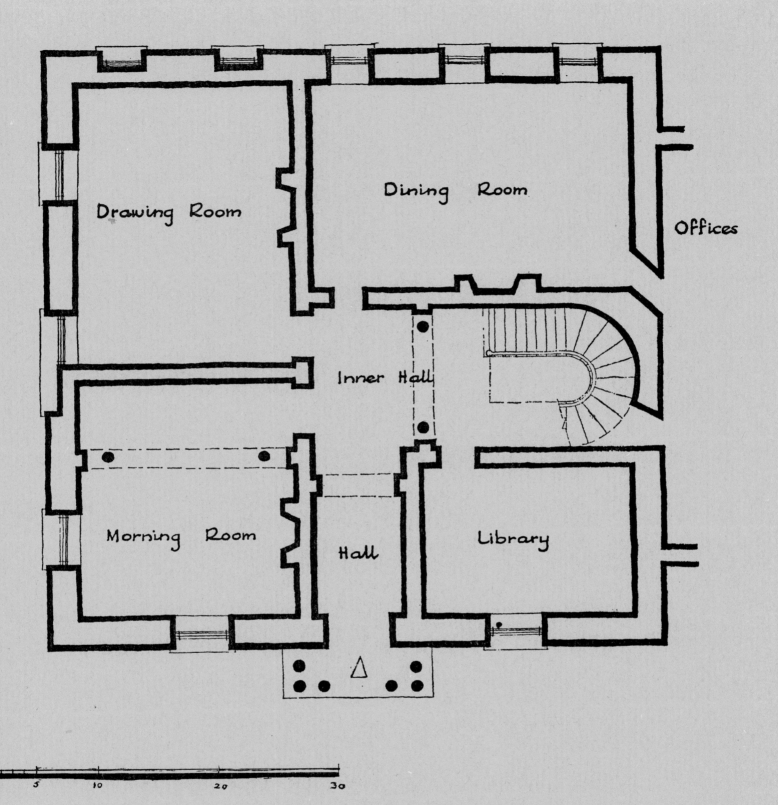

Drawing Room

Dining Room

Offices

Inner Hall

Morning Room

Hall

Library

PLAN 10 — LLYSNEWYDD

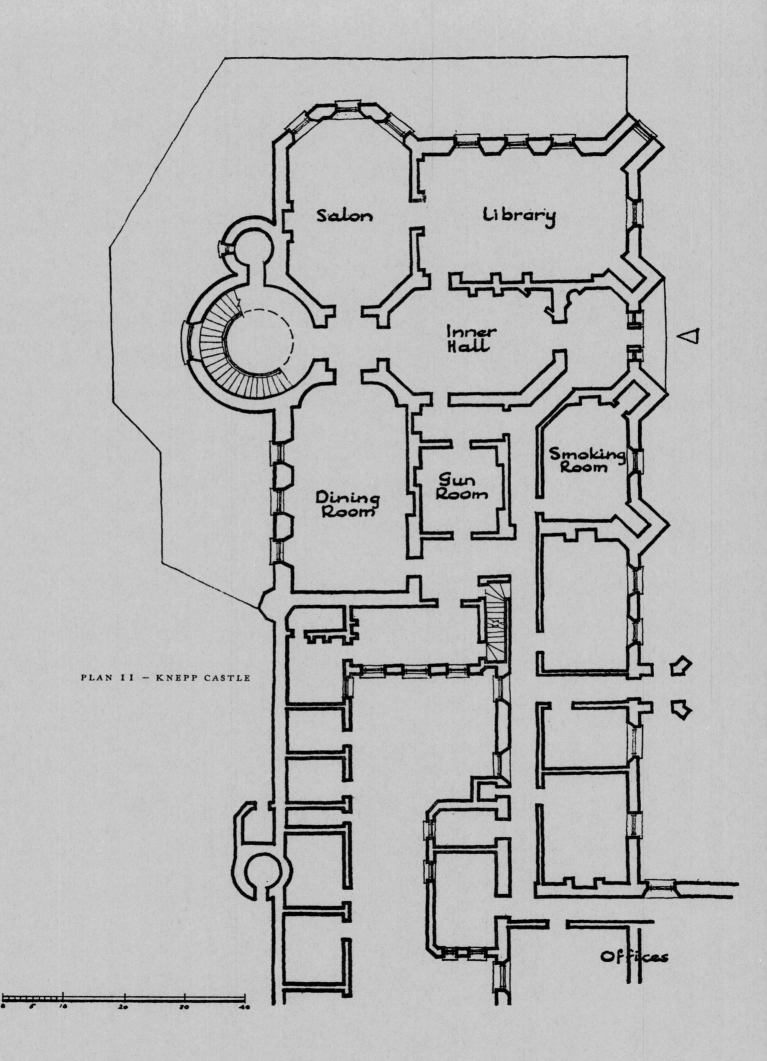

Salon

Library

Inner
Hall

Dining
Room

Gun
Room

Smoking
Room

PLAN II — KNEPP CASTLE

Offices

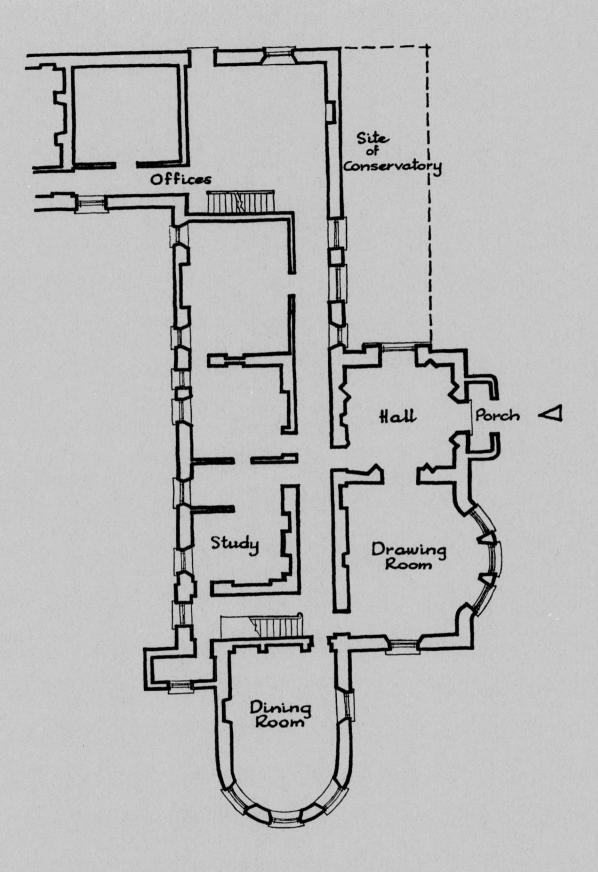

Offices

Site
of
Conservatory

Hall   Porch

Study

Drawing
Room

Dining
Room

PLAN 12 — SANDRIDGE PARK

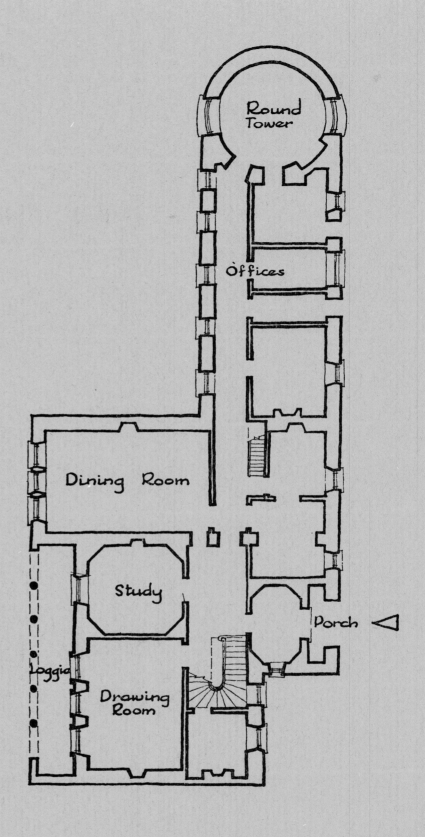

Round
Tower

Offices

Dining Room

Study

Porch

Loggia

Drawing
Room

PLAN 13 — LISSAN RECTORY

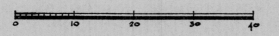

0   10   20   30   40

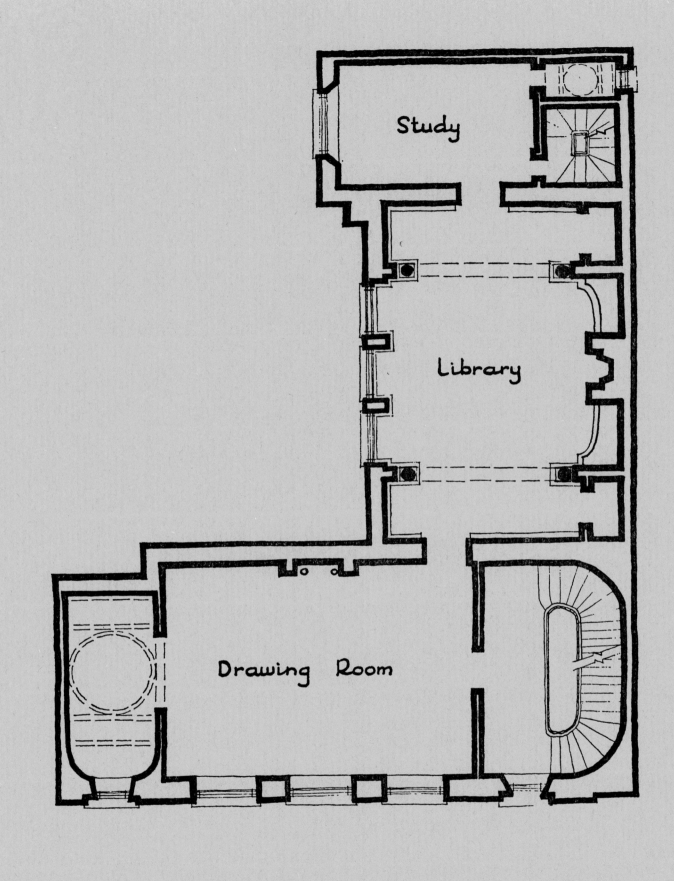

Study

Library

Drawing Room

PLAN I4 — 29 DOVER STREET

0   5   10   20   30

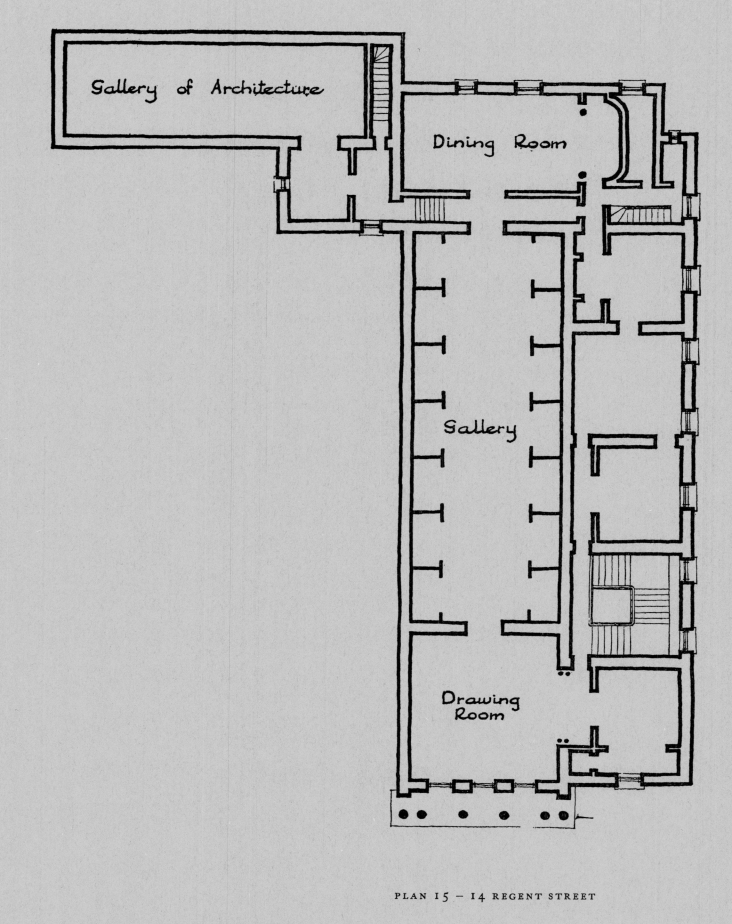

Gallery of Architecture

Dining Room

Gallery

Drawing Room

PLAN 15 — 14 REGENT STREET

0   10   20   30   40